The
100–Day
Devotional
for Men

The
100–Day
Devotional
for Men

Glenn Hascall

BARBOUR
PUBLISHING

Print ISBN 978-1-63609-454-0

Published by Barbour Publishing, Inc., 1810 Barbour Drive, Uhrichsville, Ohio 44683, www.barbourbooks.com

Our mission is to inspire the world with the life-changing message of the Bible.

Member of the
Evangelical Christian
Publishers Association

Printed in China.

This Is the Perfect Way for You to Spend Your Next 100 Days.

The 100-Day Devotional for Men offers relatable, real-life wisdom and inspiration for everyday living. On every single page, you'll encounter biblical truths you can apply to every area of your life, and you'll be encouraged—each day—to grow in your faith and spend regular time in the heavenly Father's presence.

Topics include:

> Family
> Courage
> Culture
> Stress
> Wisdom
> Priorities
> Strength
> and more!

Be blessed!

DAY 1
It Begins with a Whisper

After the earthquake there was a fire, but the
LORD was not in the fire. And after the fire
there was the sound of a gentle whisper.
1 KINGS 19:12 NLT

Above are the first words you'll read in this one-hundred-day journey. You're here, but you might not be sure what to expect. Did you begin in a moment of silence? Could you hear the pages as you opened the book? Can you hear your breath or the squeak of your chair? Perhaps this is a time before others wake or after they go to sleep, or maybe this moment is even more intentional. Where you are and what you're experiencing at this very moment could be more "earthquake and fire," making it hard to hear God's whisper.

The madness of external noise and the confusion of internal mayhem make it hard to hear God. You know you should give more than half of your available attention, but life's earthquakes and fires are distracting and somehow impressive. They insist you pay attention to them. You can't seem to take your eyes off the sight and your ears away from the sound of the blaze and shaking so you can connect with God's whisper.

But you want to. You know you need to. God wants you to listen. In the moments where noise is your normal, silence is almost painful. It's true, isn't it? All available space gets filled with sound. Earbuds, headphones, sound bars, television, radio, podcasts, or a busy coffee shop will satisfy your need for immediate noise. And yet God invites you to come away from your audio security blanket and *listen to Him whisper* healing to your soul, instructions to your mind, and kindness to your heart.

Don't miss God's words. Perhaps He'll speak here. Maybe He already has. A personal passageway to a greater friendship with God begins with a whisper and starts with knowing that every distraction makes it harder to listen, harder to hear, and harder to pay attention long enough to understand the full message He has for you. Lean in for God's whisper. Communicating with you is important to Him.

It seems like my life has an audio soundtrack, Father. There's always something begging for my attention, and I'm willing to accommodate whatever is loud. Yet You come to me in the quiet and You ask me to listen, to focus, to follow. I've missed what You've had to say far too often. Bend my ears to Your whisper.

DAY 2
No Control over the Terms

My friends, I don't feel I have already arrived.
But I forget what is behind, and I struggle for what
is ahead. I run toward the goal, so I can win the
prize of being called to heaven. This is the prize God
offers because of what Christ Jesus has done.
PHILIPPIANS 3:13–14 CEV

You have a destination. It's not where you once were, and it's someplace different than where you are right now. You exist in a place called *struggle*, and it's a place you recognize. Don't stop and wallow in the struggle. Use hard days and challenging times to remind you that if you're not where you need to be, then this is a horrible time to stop. So, keep moving. Keep following. Keep praying.

The prize isn't given in the middle of the race. But once the race is finished? That's a different story. The prize isn't given because you made the choice to run. If you get off track and run a different direction, you'll miss the finish line, where the prize is located.

Claiming the prize mentioned in the book of Philippians has nothing to do with you running, but it has everything to do with Jesus. He sponsored the race and paid for your prize. So run because you have a destination (heaven) and there's a prize waiting (life forever with God).

Today's verse has a lot packed into it, but nowhere did you read that the race is easy. Consider these three things: 1) in this race you're not finished yet, 2) what's ahead will involve struggle, and 3) you have no control over the terms of the race.

You accepted the terms of the race when you started the journey, and God makes sure the terms are satisfied. You might have looked for better terms or for a shortcut. You might even have believed for a time that you did find better terms, but the promises were false and the outcome dismal. The only thing these other terms have succeeded in doing is letting you down and sidetracking you from the real race.

Stop looking for anything other than God. It will never be God plus anything else. It will never be gold stars and achievement reports. And it never will be easy, but the struggle is worth it.

*I will need Your encouragement in this race, God.
Keep pointing the way and making sure I know where
to walk. I recognize the struggle, but it's nothing
compared to the future You've planned for me.*

DAY 3
The Dazzlers and the Definite

Watch out for people who try to dazzle you with big words and intellectual double-talk. They want to drag you off into endless arguments that never amount to anything. They spread their ideas through the empty traditions of human beings and the empty superstitions of spirit beings. But that's not the way of Christ.

Colossians 2:8 msg

Pick up a newspaper, click a few links on your favorite device, ask for opinions when you're getting coffee. . . The advice you receive will come from many perspectives, and it will rarely be as helpful as you need it to be.

This isn't uncommon. Consider a few predictions that failed to be realized. Henry Ford's attorney advised the automaker to save as much as he could because cars would only be a temporary means of transportation. Phones and TVs were also claimed to be passing fads. Thomas Edison was sure that the primary building material of the future would be steel rather than wood. Each prediction had a lot of thought put into it before it was voiced, but each was wrong.

The best human prediction will only be correct if certain unknown factors line up, but when you need predictions that are *promises without guesswork*, then don't listen to people. Only God has the correct answers because He holds the future. He never has to guess.

Today's verse describes the ideas of people as dazzling. Some people sound so smart and can counter so many arguments that you believe they know what they're talking about and that their advice has remarkable value. You might even say something like, "If they said it, then it has to be true."

The words of these dazzlers can be convincing, especially when they convince many others to follow. The number of people who believe something can make it seem like you're making a mistake if you don't agree with them. But God has never been wrong, so when He offers instruction, speaks a promise, or delivers truth, it shouldn't matter what people say. The dazzlers *could* be right—God *can't* be wrong.

Spend more time with *God the definite* and less time with *uncertain dazzlers*. There's a big difference between absolute truth and creative storytelling.

I don't need to disbelieve everything I hear or read, Father, but I need to make sure I know what You have to say about this moment and the future. You want me to check Your truth against anything people might say. You don't want me dazzled by the words of others. You want me to rest in You, assured that what You've said can be fully trusted and forever followed.

DAY 4
When I Have No Words

The Holy Spirit helps us where we are weak.
We do not know how to pray or what we should
pray for, but the Holy Spirit prays to God for us
with sounds that cannot be put into words.

ROMANS 8:26 NLV

Imagine a man working on a ranch. The back of his battered truck is loaded with posts and a roll of barbed wire. A post-hole digger or even an auger will help him get the work done, but sweat will be involved. Muscles will rebel. But as the ranch hand sticks with it, he will reach a point when the work becomes a rhythm, and he is motivated to keep going, keep working.

Many jobs are like this. Your first day on any new job can feel like the hardest work you've ever done. It's new, unfamiliar, and there's nothing routine about it. It's an odd place that hovers between a *gut it out* determination and the urge to quit. The first seems possible and the second is impractical. But that sense of awkwardness is real and powerfully strong.

If this is true for the work you do, then it's true for new social contacts, first dates, and—believe it or not—even your friendship with God. He wants you to talk to Him, but you can't find the words. Speaking to a God who is invisible and doesn't typically respond by speaking actual words can seem awkward. And sometimes your attempt to say something meaningful seems feeble, at best. If your tongue was a speed bump, then you'd be tripping over your words. Your mind and heart are loaded with issues, but your words can't seem to start flowing. You don't know what to say or how to say it.

Prayer is like talking to someone you can't see without the use of a phone. It seems impossible. You might say, "Dear God," and then a sigh escapes from someplace deep within, and you have no idea how to continue the conversation. The wounds are deep, the burden heavy, and the words are suddenly muted. You can't seem to start, and you shouldn't end your prayer. In that awkward moment, God's Spirit prays your prayer for you—perfectly, wonderfully, and mercifully. You'll learn to pray, but when you *can't*, God's Spirit prays a better prayer for you.

I pray this prayer because it's written for me, God. I want my heart to be heard, and I want to learn how to have a conversation with You. When I can't find the words to pray, please know and understand my heart.

DAY 5
Curing Insecurity

Though you have not seen him, you love him; and even though you do not see him now, you believe in him and are filled with an inexpressible and glorious joy.

1 PETER 1:8 NIV

In moments when you're all alone, you might discover your mind flooded with feelings of insecurity. It starts as a slow erosion of strength but then fills every available space. You hate these feelings because they scream, *You are not enough!* For just once you'd like to feel as if there's meaning and purpose to your life. You desperately want to be enough, but you've never been convinced that you are.

God is the answer to the questions: "What if there is more? What if there is something better? What if I'm not really alone?" He's the answer for a lot of reasons, but perhaps the biggest reason is that you'll always feel cheated or less than complete without this connection to God. He made you; He loves you; and He has planned your next great adventure. He can make you secure.

Loneliness is a common feeling. You don't feel accepted; prayer is awkward; and you're certain that the best there will ever be is some brief moment from your past. Without God, it's easy to be a cynic who looks for even just a moment of happiness but ends up empty and unfulfilled. And so expectations decrease, and so does life satisfaction. People let you down, and personal failure seems an everyday occurrence. You want to find a way forward, but all the roads you've tried have led you to nowhere good.

When you accept that God is the answer to the more you need, the better you long for, and the desire for friendship, something changes. A new path opens—one you hadn't seen before and one you've never walked. You get a solid introduction to trust; you believe without the need to see God; and there's a joy that displaces the cynic who once thought there was no one who could accept you, no need to pray, and that the good old days were gone.

God takes your insecurity and whispers, "Follow Me. There's a better day to come." And in that moment, you sidestep insecurity and take secure steps into the unknown with a God who knows where you should be going.

No one likes to admit they're insecure, Father. Yet You know my circumstances, my mind, and my excuses better than I'll ever admit. Take my insecurities and replace them with a security that only You can offer—a security I must accept—a security I've always needed.

DAY 6
Broken and Crushed

The LORD is close to the brokenhearted;
he rescues those whose spirits are crushed.
PSALM 34:18 NLT

No one gets exactly what they want and when they want it every day of their life. We will have disappointments along the way. People will interfere with our plans, and good days can go bad quickly even if we're not at fault.

There's a rumor going around that Christians who follow God should expect nothing but good things. The definition of *good things* can vary from person to person, but it's often linked to good health, lots of money, and a life of comfort and ease. The sense is that if you turn your back on God, then you can't expect any of these blessings—but some people who don't follow God have good health, lots of money, and an easy life. *Confused much?*

Sometimes Christians get by with less, struggle with health, and seem to face trouble on a regular basis. So, does God only love people who *feel* or can *prove* they've been blessed?

Brokenhearted people may not think they're blessed, but God has promised to stay close to them—and *that's* a blessing. People with crushed spirits are promised rescue. Doesn't it sound like God loves broken and crushed people?

Bad things happen to all people. It doesn't matter if they're good, bad, or simply trying hard—bad things *will* happen. That's the struggle, isn't it? Before you can come to grips with an answer, you need to understand that God loves all people who live in a broken world. Society seems to insist on breaking others. *Light bulb moment here*: that's why God stays close to those who face daily impacts from the society they live in. That's you, your family, and everyone you know. All are impacted by people who choose to break God's rules. Their decisions can and will negatively impact others.

Since trouble is a guarantee, accept help from the God who promises help to the struggler. What God promises is to take every bad day with its horrible moments and turn it into a memory that recalls how God took you from a broken moment to a moment when you experience love and security. God doesn't love you on only good days!

Sometimes it feels like my bad days are a punishment from You, God. Sure, they could be a consequence of breaking one of Your rules, but they could be damage from someone else's bad choice. Help me remember that You choose to be close to me when I struggle.

DAY 7
Yokes and Burden Relief

"If you are tired from carrying heavy burdens,
come to me and I will give you rest. Take the yoke I
give you. Put it on your shoulders and learn from me.
I am gentle and humble, and you will find rest.
This yoke is easy to bear, and this burden is light."
MATTHEW 11:28–30 CEV

You don't need a book to tell you that life is messy, but here goes: "Life is messy." You get it, you've seen it, and you've lived it. What ever happened to *best-case scenarios*? When was the last time one of those worked out for you? Been awhile?

It's possible you've lived with worst-case scenarios for as long as you can remember. You've almost come to expect it. You face a pileup of bills, health issues, job crises, and family dysfunction. Some issues you share with a close circle of friends, but most you keep to yourself. They're burdens you can't get rid of. Or can you? . . .

First of all, you should know that the struggles you face are not entirely new and strange. Others have faced similar issues. The wisest among all these *others* have taken all the struggle that has accumulated and made the choice to take their problems to God and leave them in His perfectly capable hands. They humbly say something like "I don't know what You're going to do with this, but I don't want it, can't use it, and I'm tired of carrying it." And the thing they don't want, can't use, and don't need is taken by a good—no, *great!*—God.

When you give your struggles to God, He gives you a yoke in return. (A yoke is a device farmers use to connect two animals together to make the work easier.) You still get to be involved, but God does the hard work, and He always leads. He's not going to be pushy or a harsh taskmaster. He'll simply help you get the work done. He knows where to go. And because you're linked with Him, you go where He goes. The only way this arrangement becomes difficult is if you resist going His direction. He will remain gentle, but He's wiser than you are and knows where you should be going and why it's important to go there. He patiently waits for you to learn to walk with Him.

I'm beginning to think that somehow You really do understand me, Father. You are uniquely You—and I'll never be exactly like You, but You understand me and want me to walk willingly with You. Help me resist being stubborn along the way.

DAY 8
Trouble's Expiration Date

*These hard times are small potatoes compared to the
coming good times, the lavish celebration prepared
for us. There's far more here than meets the eye.
The things we see now are here today, gone tomorrow.
But the things we can't see now will last forever.*
2 Corinthians 4:17–18 msg

Gnats are insects that annoy people to no end. They're less than a quarter inch in length; they can't fly very well; and they're always where you don't want them to be. Some might say these insect irritations are small potatoes compared to much of the time when they don't bug you. But, for some reason, you remember the gnat longer than you should.

The Bible says you will experience issues that annoy you, trouble your mind, and cause you to become frustrated. The Word doesn't say they aren't big deals, but they're forgettable when compared to the forever life Christians get to experience with God in heaven.

As we've seen in the last few devotions, all of this world's mess serves a very important purpose. You might need to know that every human life is filled with struggle. Maybe you need to know you're not alone in dealing with struggle. Everyone needs to know that humans are flawed, and life is hard. This isn't, in any way, meant to discourage you. In fact, it's to remind you (or help you understand for the first time) that there's a way to deal with the struggle you face. You can't be encouraged in little things if you don't believe God takes care of the big stuff.

There will always be more to your struggle than you can see. God is doing things you're unaware of. If trouble comes, then it will eventually go. It will never be allowed to set up a permanent address at your house. Even if trouble stays for longer than you'd like, your permanent address is in heaven with God. And trouble isn't allowed there.

Think of all the things you have to do to prepare for a family reunion. There's inconvenience, there's a to-do list to complete, and you might even have to interact with people who aren't very nice. Then, when the reunion happens, memories are made that will last a lifetime. How much more impressive do you think heaven will be? Like the gnat, trouble always comes—but it has an expiration date.

Help me remember that no matter what I face, You face it with me, and there will be a day when You banish all trouble, God. I look forward to that day. Give me the patience I need in this waiting room called life.

DAY 9
No Separation Required

I know that nothing can keep us from the love of God.
Death cannot! Life cannot! Angels cannot! Leaders cannot!
Any other power cannot! Hard things now or in the future
cannot! The world above or the world below cannot!
Any other living thing cannot keep us away from the love
of God which is ours through Christ Jesus our Lord.
ROMANS 8:38–39 NLV

Are you convinced that God's love is always available? Or do you think it's possible that there are things that can come between you and God's love? Believe it or not, some people think that if they break just one more of God's rules, then God won't want anything more to do with them. They feel like their next choice could leave them wearing the name tag: LOST CAUSE or BROKEN BEYOND REPAIR.

This common belief adds to feelings of insecurity. You may already believe that people can't be trusted. You might even believe that you can't be trusted, and then you feel like you're just one bad decision away from being rejected by God. Who wants that? Who needs that? . . .

Today's verses plainly state that there's *nothing* that can put any distance between your need and God's love. If His love were a concert, you'd receive an all-access pass. If it were a phone service, your calls would always go through. In an emergency, you'd be top priority. There's no hesitation, no waiting, and no end to His love. There's never a demand to buy or earn that love. There's no layaway or installment program. You only get two choices: accept His love or reject it.

How would you need to rearrange your thinking about God if you truly believed that His love is available anytime and anywhere? Would believing that God really loves you make you feel more secure? How would your perception of God be altered? How would you see yourself differently?

It's possible to find yourself separated from God; but in that case, it would always be because *you* made the choice to step away from Him. But God keeps the door wide open for you to step back in so your journey with Him can continue.

With God there's no separation, no decrease in His love, and no taking back His offer.

I want to trust that You love me, Father. I want to believe nothing can separate me from Your love. I want to have faith in Your promises. This means I need to believe I can be loved and that Your love is the only thing that can make me secure.

DAY 10
Things God Will Not Do

*"The LORD himself goes before you and will be
with you; he will never leave you nor forsake you.
Do not be afraid; do not be discouraged."*
DEUTERONOMY 31:8 NIV

If you can't go to any place where God is not, then the best conclusion is that God goes with you everywhere you go. He never leaves; He doesn't race ahead while you lag behind; and He doesn't give up on you. His Spirit lives in you so He can work through you.

One of the biggest struggles in life is the feeling that you're alone—but if you're a Christian, then *your perception* of loneliness is not reality. This false perception could be caused by a personal unwillingness to share your burden with God. The reality is that you can carry a burden as long as you'd like, but God still asks you to let it go and allow Him to take care of things. If you don't give it to Him, you may feel like you're living life alone—but that's a decision you've made.

Think of social media for a minute. You get to choose who can see your posts. The things you share are distributed to an audience you choose. Your relationship with God is the same way. You can keep information private and not share your status update with God, even if you share it with others. The truth is, nothing is ever hidden from God, so He knows the truth about you even if you refuse to tell Him.

What would be an acceptable reason to try to hide your story from God? There is no good reason. But one reason may be easier to understand than others: fear. You may feel that familiar sense of insecurity that tries to convince you that God has every right to abandon you and that He's close to leaving you. This faulty thinking can cause you to be a hypocrite with God. You try to make it sound as though you don't need His help because you're making great choices that don't involve breaking His rules.

God knows the reality of your life because He lives within you. He hears what you say, knows what you think, and pays attention to what you do. You don't get to hide *anything* from Him. And even knowing all the things you've gotten wrong, He will not leave. He will not race ahead while you lag behind, and He will not give up on you.

Thanks for sticking with imperfect me, God. I want to be
open and honest about my failures so You can make the
changes I need to experience the freedom to obey You.

DAY 11
Breaking God Laws

Oh, what a miserable person I am! Who will free me
from this life that is dominated by sin and death?
Thank God! The answer is in Jesus Christ our Lord. So you
see how it is: In my mind I really want to obey God's law,
but because of my sinful nature I am a slave to sin.

ROMANS 7:24–25 NLT

The reason misery loves company is that it wants to compare misery scars with the misery scars of others. Somehow you can make a competition out of things that make you miserable. Sad, but true. Most misery comes from poor personal decision-making. After all, if you'd just apply a little more willpower, an extra dose of self-discipline, and a steady supply of determination, you should be able to resist letting yourself, other people, and God down, right?

The choice to sin (to break God's laws) seems as natural as breathing. You can make poor choices without a second thought. Sinning is easy—it's often a person's first response. So, if you sin but don't want to sin and have tried to stop sinning without success, how do you experience the freedom to make better choices? The answer is found in a friendship with Jesus.

He can take all the *want to* you've bottled up inside and trade His strength for your weakness. That should be an everyday trade.

You'll never be able to take the personal choice to make God-like decisions and have a perfect track record if you only use your own perseverance. Without God's help, you'll fail—repeatedly.

By trying to help God out by not bugging Him, you actually set yourself up for additional failure. He's with you; He doesn't leave you; and His help is the only thing that gives you the freedom to say no to breaking His laws. The alternative is to remain in bondage to a cycle that starts with only your determination, refuses God's help, and ends with sin. The aftermath includes frustration, hiding, and insecurity. Stop trying to avoid sin on your own. God understands, and He knows how you can avoid it.

Tomorrow you'll discover why going to God for help should be a decision you never hesitate to make.

You can help me, and I need help, Father. You have strength, and I need Your strength. You have answers, and I need Your answers. May You be my first call and not my last resort. There's no one who can do what You can. Turning to You is always my best response.

DAY 12
No Black Clouds

*With the arrival of Jesus, the Messiah, that fateful
dilemma is resolved. Those who enter into Christ's being-
here-for-us no longer have to live under a continuous,
low-lying black cloud. A new power is in operation.
The Spirit of life in Christ, like a strong wind, has
magnificently cleared the air, freeing you from a fated
lifetime of brutal tyranny at the hands of sin and death.*
ROMANS 8:1–2 MSG

There was a time when people tried to please God by giving
a lot of personal effort. When they failed, they felt bad, and
many would give up on the idea. God kept calling them to
come back to Him, but they were wanderers, and wandering
became their favorite pastime.

God could judge them for breaking His rules because
that's what they chose to do. The people were not capable of
continuously following God. They got off-track. Their verdict
read, "Guilty!"

People had shown how unfaithful they could be to God.
Would He retaliate? Would mankind be punished for being
wanderers? Like children, the people had shown themselves
lovable but too willing to do the wrong thing. A spiritual
time-out was common for these rule-breakers, but it wasn't
enough—and a time-out wasn't a permanent solution.

Sin had abused people long enough. So, God sent Jesus to do something about it. This mission would result in a once-and-for-all ending to the totalitarian rule of sin. There's no doubt sin can still be persuasive, but its ultimate power is toothless. Its bite doesn't have to be fatal.

Jesus took possession of every sin that *had ever been* committed. He gathered every sin that *would ever be* committed. He took the "Guilty!" verdict on Himself for every one of those sins (including yours!) when He died on the cross. Your breaking of God's rules can result in a heavenly verdict of "Not Guilty!" and no condemnation if you confess your sins and receive His forgiveness. Jesus didn't stay dead. He's alive and ready to help you learn how to live the victorious life you never could live on your own.

If you think it no longer matters to God whether you break His rules, then you should know how much it cost Him to make sure nothing stands in your way of being close to Him. He still wants obedience, but He wants to walk with you as someone forgiven and loved and not someone who feels guilty and rejected. He thinks you're worth it.

Thanks for paying a sin debt You didn't owe, God.
Your Son satisfied the demand for justice, and I get
to walk with You today loved, forgiven, and without
condemnation. Let this good news keep changing me.

DAY 13
Aging Stronger

We never give up. Our bodies are gradually dying,
but we ourselves are being made stronger each day.
2 CORINTHIANS 4:16 CEV

Someone once said that good health is, at best, the slowest rate of dying. A cartoon character once said that no matter how you look at it, no one gets out of this world alive. Death is a common experience. Everyone who is born will also die.

If that sounds morbid, then consider some good news. There's a difference between your body, which will die, and your spirit and soul, which will not. Spend time strengthening the last two, because looks won't last, strength will fade, and the fountain of youth is just a nice, fictional story.

The last thing God wants is for you to give up, but that desire isn't linked with doing everything you can to live longer. *Don't give up.* There will be a lot of living *after* your body gives out. The decisions you make here and now prepare you for forever.

Many people struggle with the idea of death. It's likely not because they don't want God's future—they may even be more than willing to be in His presence. But death is something they have no personal experience with, and the unknown, the points of transition from life to death to eternity can seem scary.

Your spirit and soul can gain strength when your body is losing a grip on the things it was once able to do. The life you're living right now provides the transition from struggle to a place where fear isn't welcome, tears are banished, and pain is past tense—for all eternity!

This isn't a doom and gloom message. This is profound encouragement. Consider something missionary Jim Elliot said about death: "He is no fool who gives what he cannot keep to gain what he cannot lose."

Don't fall so in love with your life here that you don't prepare well for forever. God's instructions are for today but have lots to do with tomorrow. He can help shift your thinking from what you plan to do next weekend to what it will be like finally to be where God is. This is the God who made your body to be temporary but your spirit and soul permanent.

A slowing body is just another opportunity to age stronger in the things God made to be strong.

I want to become more concerned about my future, Father.
Help me remember who You are, what You've done, and
how You're preparing for everything that is yet to come.

DAY 14
God Works Full-Time

*We are His work. He has made us to belong to Christ Jesus so
we can work for Him. He planned that we should do this.*
Ephesians 2:10 nlv

It took six days for God to create the world and all it contains.
He created planets, the sun, stars, universes, and galaxies.
On the seventh day, He rested. From this impressive start,
God made mankind His work—and He's never given up
the job. He created an extensive manual of life instructions
and sent messengers to make His rules clear to people who
seem confused.

God's plan has always been to help humans connect
with Him. He wants harmony between His plan and your
response. A few days ago, you read that Jesus came to do what
you could not. God sent Jesus to be the main character in
His best news—mankind's rescue.

You are not someone God needs to be reminded about. He
doesn't care for you on a part-time basis. His love isn't offered
as part of a timeshare. He patiently works with you, on you,
and for you, every moment of your life. He won't make you
do anything you don't want to do, but He will provide all the
reasons why walking in His footsteps is the very best choice.

God does the work because it's His plan for you to become His ambassador. You'll always have an opportunity

to share what you know about God with people who have been ignoring the work He is doing. God isn't just trying to get free labor; His message is so big, so transforming, and so important that He needs all hands on deck to share it. God wants others to see the change He has made in you and to hear your salvation story.

If God can do the work to pull your spiritual feet from the muck of sin, then why would you leave others to think that breaking free from the same thing is little more than wishful thinking?

Yesterday you learned that there's a future, and it offers nothing that you need to be afraid of. God created this life for you, and He's working to make you fit for the future He has planned. He wants you to be willing to work to share His good news and to have a desire to stay close to Jesus.

Your work has brought me close, God. Your Good News keeps me sharing with others. Your future keeps me longing for home. Thank You for the work You do that helps me understand that there will never be anything in my life that could be more important than a relationship with You.

The Cause—The Effect

For it is by grace you have been saved, through faith—and this is not from yourselves, it is the gift of God—not by works, so that no one can boast.

Ephesians 2:8–9 NIV

If you get a promotion at work, you can usually pinpoint the work ethic, the decisions, and the track record that contributed to it. A promotion means greater prestige, more income, and vaster responsibility. It may sound strange to you, but this cause and effect is *not* the way things work in God's kingdom. God has already done the work Himself.

It will never be your effort that does anything to improve God's opinion of you. He loves you already, and that won't change. He walks with you, and that will never change. Nothing you do or don't do will affect any of His promises.

You don't get to put a certificate on the wall saying that you did all the work that got you to God's graduation ceremony. If you make your relationship with God all about the things you've done, then you're missing the point. This relationship is only possible because of what God did. It may be tempting to talk about all the things you've done for God, but are you as willing to list all the things He has done for you?

How do you know when you've done enough to graduate? Are some good works worth more to God than others? It is true that God has rules to follow. It's also true that He will help when it's most difficult to follow those rules. But the life rescue He offers is an unearned gift that will never depend on your best work ethic.

God created a rescue plan that He could administer from start to finish. This plan would only be dependent on what He could do, so there would never be a question about who were the rescued and who was the Rescuer.

He knew you would need someone to save you from your worst self, so He willingly did what needed to be done to rescue and redeem those who can't save themselves.

You won't love me more if I spend more time being busy, Father. You won't love me less either. I want to appreciate the work that only You can do and then obey, because I want to be part of Your plan. And even when work and obedience seem like the same thing, help me learn that the difference is that You do all the work and then ask me to obey.

DAY 16
Life without Confusion

All Scripture is inspired by God and is useful to teach us what is true and to make us realize what is wrong in our lives. It corrects us when we are wrong and teaches us to do what is right. God uses it to prepare and equip his people to do every good work.

2 Timothy 3:16–17 NLT

Some books seem like nothing more than random ramblings of a distracted mind. The Bible is not one of those books. The thoughts, instructions, worship, and examples all have something important to teach you. The Bible is the primary way God will answer your questions about everything—from the choices you make to the things you believe.

God's Word helps you know what to pursue and what to avoid. It defines the differences between right and wrong, good and bad, and what helps and what hurts.

It's not especially hard to feel as though, when it comes to living the Christian life, you're in over your head. There can be a disconnect between what you assume to be true and what God says is true. Those things may be different. You might not know the truth because you haven't spent time reading the Truth.

God gives Christians the opportunity to do something amazing, yet many wait around not knowing what to do and not knowing that God can equip them for anything He asks them to do. Maybe you've experienced that sense of confusion. God doesn't want you to be confused. Remember that He sent His Spirit to teach, His Word to connect your belief to His truth, and His Son to bring this connected life to those who would welcome the instruction.

If the Bible were little more than inspiring memes and memorable stories, it would mean people would pick it up, read it once (or wait for the movie release), and have warm feelings about posting about the idea of faith on social media. But God's Word does more than that. It's worth reading repeatedly because you'll discover something new with every read.

Don't be confused. You can know God's heart, and this knowing starts with the reading of the words He wrote.

You know everything I don't, God. Make plain the truth
that I consider complicated. Make it clear to my mind,
pleasing to my soul, and motivational to my decision-making.
You don't leave me in the dark. Your light shines through
Your Word. Help me to read it, understand it, and live it.

Public Demonstrations?

Is it not clear to you that to go back to that old rule-keeping, peer-pleasing religion would be an abandonment of everything personal and free in my relationship with God? I refuse to do that, to repudiate God's grace. If a living relationship with God could come by rule-keeping, then Christ died unnecessarily.

GALATIANS 2:21 MSG

The Pharisees were the best that religion seemed to offer. They knew the rules; they kept the rules; and they couldn't wait to pay for space on a billboard to tell you they were better than you. The problem was they didn't just pay attention to the rules because they wanted to be closer to God. They followed the rules so they could compare themselves with anyone who didn't keep the rules as well as they did. They were the kings of achievement reports, and they had no problem arrogantly putting down others who didn't measure up.

This was the common public demonstration of the link between mankind and God before Jesus came. It was never sanctioned by God, as if religion was a blood sport and people just needed the chance to prove they were better than their fellow human beings. But there were others who wanted to impress the Pharisees more than they wanted to please God. They sought affirmation from people who routinely looked down on them, and some of those who looked down were certain God loved them more.

Then God sent along some great news. People don't have to try to impress Him, impress others, or buy friendships by making human opinions more important than His.

If you could save or rescue your own life by keeping rules, then why would there be any need for the supreme sacrifice Jesus offered for you when He died in your place and then rose from the dead to claim victory over the grave?

When you commit your life to Christ, your spiritual world opens to a flood of freedom. You're free to follow God, to accept His opinion of you, and to realize that the death of Jesus Christ sets you free from opinion polls. You can and should be authentic. Follow Christ. Believe that He really does love you and can transform your sinful nature to obedience that responds with love, because He first loved you.

You say I'm free to follow You, Father. Help me with that. I get weary trying to live up to the expectations of people who aren't You. Then I fail to look to You for the compassion I need. Help me to see Your friendship as the most important friendship I will ever have.

DAY 18
God's "Hope" Words

The Scriptures were written to teach and
encourage us by giving us hope.
ROMANS 15:4 CEV

How appealing would the Bible be if it simply told you that you're doing everything wrong and there's no hope for you? While it may be true that you're doing things that don't line up with God's plans for you, and it may be true that you believe you're beyond God's help, it's equally true that the Bible teaches what's right and shares news that turns despair into hope, remorse into joy, distance into closeness. You've experienced the old life, but God wants you to experience something new.

The Bible is the bestselling book of all time. It's not hard to believe this is true. Yet people act as though God is just waiting to catch you making a mistake so He can punish you and make life little more than living misery. When you read the Bible, you'll get an entirely different picture of God. His teachings provide practical reasons for making a life change, but that change is dependent on your willingness to offer Him your trust.

Every person can expect death at the end of life, *but* God offers life at the end of death—and that's real hope. It gets more amazing the longer you think about it. He's offering you something no one else has or will be able to offer. If someone else does promise this, they can't deliver. God is called "Faithful and True." He sent Jesus to buy you back from sin's pawn shop. That's called *redemption*, and everyone needs it.

Imagine attempting to read the Bible if God were portrayed as cold, unmoved by human need, and vindictive. Spend time actually exploring the words He wrote. His greatest attribute is love, and one of His greatest virtues is mercy. Accept His love and be grateful for His mercy, because they're the truth you need. No human is guilt-free, but God promises to trade you His forgiveness for your guilt. Read His words, be encouraged, discover joy.

Saying that I know You without reading Your Word only leaves me guessing, God. My opinions can be swayed by what other people think and by what I assume to be true. Help me discover the You that shows up in the Bible. Give me the hope I need for life today and the forever life You promise those who are willing to count on, and refuse to live without, Your rescue.

DAY 19
Priority Won

*Let God change your life. First of all, let Him give you a
new mind. Then you will know what God wants you to do.
And the things you do will be good and pleasing and perfect.*

ROMANS 12:2 NLV

There's no end to five-step programs that promise a better you.
They suggest you can have better health, better relationships,
better employment, and better parenting. You pick the topic,
and there's someone, somewhere who can give you steps to
make things better in that area of your life.

The Bible offers a one-step plan: "Let God change your
life." Why make it harder than God intended? Recognize that
He can make the primary change in your life—if you let Him.
His Spirit lives in your heart, but the change happens first
in your mind. This is where you reason whether God can be
trusted and determine if you believe He can rescue. Then your
faith will give God the green light to transform your mind.

You'll need that change if you're going to understand
that there are some very specific things God wants you to
do. Once you understand that, then there is no good reason
not to obey what God wants. And if you do what God asks
you to do, it will be good, pleasing, and perfect.

This first step is laid out in a very straightforward way in
Romans. You don't need to become a better person before

putting your trust in the God who can make you a better person. You don't need to clean up your poor decision-making history to allow God to help you make great decisions. You don't have to guess what God wants, because God tells you in His Word.

So, stop wasting time trying to be the best you *before* you come to God. Only He can make you a new creation in Christ (2 Corinthians 5:17).

Let God's priority for your life win. If you're not lining up with what God wants for you, then let Him start with your thinking. Learn the value of obedience. Do what is good for you, pleasing to Him, and perfectly aligned with His priorities for you.

I can spend time doing my best to be the best for You,
Father, but You say I can't do that on my own.
I know You can change me. Help me give You the green
light. Transform me. Start with my thinking.

DAY 20
Don't Choose Distraction

Martha was distracted by all the preparations that had to be made. She came to [Jesus] and asked, "Lord, don't you care that my sister has left me to do the work by myself? Tell her to help me!" "Martha, Martha," the Lord answered, "you are worried and upset about many things, but few things are needed— or indeed only one. Mary has chosen what is better."

LUKE 10:40–42 NIV

Is your priority as a Christian to look the part or to actually be a student? Is it more important to conform to a ritual or to embrace a relationship? Did Jesus have an opinion on these subjects?

Because you read today's verses, then you know Jesus did have a preference. You could leave this passage, thinking that doing your best for God is looked down on by Him. It's not. Jesus didn't condemn Martha for wanting to deliver a quality dining experience. He merely reminded her that developing a relationship with Him, like Mary was doing, should have been her top priority.

Despite anything you might think about event planning, it seems God is more concerned about who is coming to the event and their interest in learning from Him than He is about what's on the menu and who will be planning things.

Perhaps the greatest reason God views one person's actions

more favorably than another's has to do with the difference between making a decision based on how it makes the person look and truly being devoted to Him. Do you think it makes sense to God to emphasize anything that keeps you distracted from what He's trying to teach you?

Yes, do things in the best way possible. But when service supersedes spending time in worship and you lose connection with God and are serving in your own strength, you need to reorder your priorities.

You can liken this to memories you may have of spending time with your grandpa or maybe your dad. The greatest memories, the most important lessons, the moments that exist without regret, are the ones where you were engaged with him and not those moments when you harbored the wish to be anywhere else.

I want You to be honored in what I do, God, but never at the expense of ignoring You while others enjoy Your company. Help me choose to be engaged in my time with You. I want my time with You to be a place of no regret.

DAY 21
Priority Pole Position

Jesus replied, " 'You must love the LORD your God
with all your heart, all your soul, and all your mind.'
This is the first and greatest commandment."
MATTHEW 22:37–38 NLT

The idea of a bucket list suggests that you have priorities and that the list you keep isn't complete yet. Things you need to get done today may take precedence. But one thing that should be at the very top somehow gets bumped for almost any other thing.

If God sets the first priority on your list as loving Him with every part of what makes you who you are, then how is it possible that a text, phone call, or someone saying your name in another room diverts you from priority number one? Sure, you'll get back to it, or so you tell yourself. . .but one priority after another fights for that top spot, and God gets moved farther down the list.

At the end of the day, you might encounter some regret only to promise yourself that tomorrow God will once again be in the top spot, and the priority pole position will do its best to prove you wrong once more.

If it weren't for God's mercy, there would be immediate and strong consequences for breaking God's greatest commandment. But this same God who knows you also knows you can only apply good intentions to your priority list, so He made it His priority to love you first, love you most, and love you before you could ever love Him in return. And through Matthew 22, He'll remind you that love is a two-way street. He's always loved you. Now love Him in return. Make that your top priority, and let God help you keep your priorities in line.

God didn't create you for a "someday relationship"; He wants you to move forward with Him today. He didn't ask for a part-time love; He wants you to respond to His full-time compassion. He doesn't give you a résumé to look over to see if He's worth it; He gave you His Word and said that connecting with Him is the greatest thing you'll ever do.

Let the "someday" that I believe will come to my relationship with You happen today, Father. Keep my mind on You and my heart set on following You. I don't want to settle for good intentions. I want to follow Your lead. I don't want to wait for some better day before I take You seriously.

DAY 22
He Did. He Is. He Will.

For everything, absolutely everything, above and below,
visible and invisible, rank after rank after rank of angels—
everything got started in him and finds its purpose in
him. He was there before any of it came into existence
and holds it all together right up to this moment.
COLOSSIANS 1:16–17 MSG

You have a brilliant idea for a new business. You have an attorney help you with paperwork, and as your business grows, you develop a human resources department to help you identify quality candidates for employment. You need department heads to manage various aspects of the business and employees to help make the business successful. That's generally how a business grows. It takes a lot of people doing a lot of things.

God didn't need that kind of organization. He had a big idea for the creation of plants, animals, and humans. They would need a place to live, so He created the earth. They would need to see, so He created the sun, moon, and stars for light. They would need hydration, so He created water to fill streams and lakes. They would need to communicate, so He created language. God considered every need mankind would ever have before the first human took his first breath. God's priority was humankind, and He needed no reminder of that and no help to take care of them.

God didn't have to create things that mankind would never see, but He did. He didn't have to create human biology in such a way that it is marvelous in its designs, but He did. He didn't have to keep taking care of what He created, but He did—and He will.

Not only did God create everything, but He insisted that life itself had value so everything He ever created would serve a purpose. Nothing was left behind in His thinking. Nothing was forgotten in His plan. *Nothing.*

God doesn't need help, but you need His help. You can start plenty of things, but can you keep at them from start to finish? Maybe not. Employers need help. So do parents, students, and children. That's everyone. God uses His Word to remind you of His priorities. Perhaps these reminders are given because to keep them straight, you must rely on God.

I need You to do what I can't, God. Teach me to
value Your priorities, and then help me keep them.
You've proven that You can start something and keep it
going without failure, faltering, or forgetfulness. Keep
working on me, and help me value what You value.

One-Thing Priority

Respect and obey God! This is what life is all about.
ECCLESIASTES 12:13 CEV

What if, in your entire existence, you chose to complete a single task? What would that task be? It's easy to think of embarking on a daring adventure, inventing something that would change lives for good, or being someone others admire and respect. What would be so important to you that it claims that "one thing" status?

When you're five years old, that one thing may seem simple and perhaps childish. There may be a time when personal ideals link you to a different goal or ambition. Your one thing may change with your circumstances, for example, when you get married, when you have children, or when you are hip deep in advancing your career.

God also has a list of priorities for you. One of the priorities God says is important is to respect and obey Him. If that's what life is all about, is this priority something that actually shows up on your "one thing" list?

Respecting someone who is really good at their job isn't difficult. They may be someone you look up to and want to be like. If they give a speech, you want to hear what they have to say. Their knowledge could help you in your career. But God already does this. He knows the key to life, and He shares it. He has answers, and He waits for your questions. Do you look up to Him? Do you want to be like Him? Do you respect Him more than any human you've even known? Do you do what He says you should do? You can make His priorities your priorities, and it'll be those revised priorities that impact every part of your life from this day forward.

When I want Your way, Father, then I get to have my way because it's only then that we both want the same thing. If I make plans and they're different from Yours, please make me aware enough to see what I should be doing when I'm also aware that I'm not walking Your path. Help me respect You. Help me obey You. Help me love You—today, tomorrow, and always.

DAY 24
The People Priority

Nothing should be done because of pride or thinking about yourself. Think of other people as more important than yourself. Do not always be thinking about your own plans only. Be happy to know what other people are doing.
PHILIPPIANS 2:3–4 NLV

If you're reviewing your mental priority list today, there's one item you should bump up and another that should be removed altogether. The one to keep is humility, and the one to get rid of is pride. They are complete opposites. Pride only cares about you. Humility cares about others. One sounds selfish, and the other sounds like a God response. Since God is your best example, give humility top billing on your priority list. The difference will be noticeable.

What if you actually cared enough about others to ask for a personal status update? What if you were actually to listen to what they have to say? What if, when the conversation is over, they feel certain that you wanted to know?

You always remember people who have done that for you. You might remember where the conversation took place, the things you discussed, and how they made you feel safe in sharing a great burden.

While this kind of response is God's idea of normal, it's not what people experience most of the time. Perhaps that's why it seems so memorable when it happens.

When someone dies, there are always memories attached to their life. Do you want to be remembered as the guy who yelled at neighbor kids to get off the lawn or as a man who knew other people by name and made them feel as if there was nothing more important than the crisis they were enduring? Your best legacy won't be based on how much stuff you could buy or how many awards you earned. This legacy happens when your priority is God and the people He loves.

People often believe no one really cares about them or for them. They've accumulated lots of evidence, and they seem to be alone in their battle. God will be there in that battle whether you step in or not, but He wants you to step in. He wants you to do things as radical as lending a hand, a listening ear, and a kind response. Make it a priority, because it's something God wants people to see in you.

You have already done for me what You ask me to do for others, God. Help me prioritize people without calling attention to my personal accomplishments. I want to be willing to listen and help in the way You think is best.

Prayers That Haven't Been Prayed

What causes fights and quarrels among you?
Don't they come from your desires that battle within
you? You desire but do not have, so you kill. You covet
but you cannot get what you want, so you quarrel and
fight. You do not have because you do not ask God.
JAMES 4:1–2 NIV

You live in a competitive world. Career advancement is often based on performance. Promotions are given to those either most capable or most willing to do what needs to be done. You might look around to see who you're competing with. The company wants teamwork, but you might want a team of one with everyone else considered a rival.

This highly competitive spirit is the backstory of today's verses. If you live in a constant battle with those who are supposed to be part of your team, then it's much easier for the actual team that opposes you to get you sidetracked. This sidetracking could be in your family, on the job, or in the church. Fights and quarrels can take a field trip to any of those three places.

Getting your own way is important when selfishness and pride become your traveling companions. You can't envision a reason to give up any ground you think you've taken. In fact, anything you think of as success can make you thirsty for more success—even if God's plan for success looks different than what you've settled for.

Because you won't see eye to eye with God, it can be easy to feel like you have to play the game and be in it to win it. But God stands by, waiting for you to ask Him for help.

Don't take what isn't yours. Don't insist you're the best. And don't forget to ask God for help. If you don't ask, how is God responsible for not answering a prayer that has never been prayed?

Scratch and claw to win, but don't be surprised when you face a struggle that doesn't bring you closer to God and moves you further away from other people.

God always has a reason for why He gives the instructions you read, and often it's very practical. If you insist on having your way, then life becomes much more lonely because you become much more isolated.

I know I need to ask You for help, Father. Too often I want to try to figure things out on my own, and it seems like everything I touch suffers. Keep my mouth from boasting, my heart from isolating, and my head from thinking I know more than You do.

DAY 26
The Faith Outlet

*I urge you, first of all, to pray for all people. Ask God to help
them; intercede on their behalf, and give thanks for them.
Pray this way for kings and all who are in authority so that
we can live peaceful and quiet lives marked by godliness
and dignity. This is good and pleases God our Savior, who
wants everyone to be saved and to understand the truth.*

1 TIMOTHY 2:1–4 NLT

Prayer seems like the time to ask God for the things you
need—*and it is*. But if that's all there is to your prayer, then
it misses the concept of faith. You see, faith is believing that a
good God with good plans can bring good to the lives of humanity. Faith is dependence on God and being dependable in
the lives of others. It is learning the value of relationships and
then using what you learn to stand with and for other people.

Prayer is a faith outlet. It gives you a place to practice
what you're learning. God loves people, and so should you.
God helps people, and so should you. God cares about the
things that concern people, and so should you. Prayer allows
you to take the needs of people around you to God. It's a gift
of love brimming with compassion. It expresses empathy and
wants God's good plans to work through the lives of those in
need. It might encourage you to help when God stands with
the needs of others. Prayer allows you to be sensitive enough
to see where God is working and then go there.

God wants to know that you're thankful for other people. Many will encourage you. Some will test your patience. *All* are God's masterpieces. He wants you to be as overwhelmed by His creation as possible. You can't do that when you feel the need to compete and compare.

When you pray for other people, you recognize that their need may be the very thing God can use to redeem and rescue them.

The prayers you pray for everyone should be for their good and God's best. Praying prayers that ask God to give them what they deserve isn't quite connected to His heart, His plan, or His future.

May I populate my prayers with names, God. I want my prayers to include more than I, me, and mine. Teach me how to care for people the way You do. Help me see them the same way You do—as people You want to rescue, not reject.

DAY 27
Unfurl the God Map

Don't fret or worry. Instead of worrying, pray. Let petitions
and praises shape your worries into prayers, letting God
know your concerns. Before you know it, a sense of God's
wholeness, everything coming together for good, will come
and settle you down. It's wonderful what happens when
Christ displaces worry at the center of your life.
PHILIPPIANS 4:6–7 MSG

Worry is only marginally useful if it helps you recognize
there's a problem. It could be something in your own life or
the life of someone you know. Worry leaves you wringing
your hands and struggling with the unknown. The problem is
too big for you, and the outcome is nowhere in sight. Worry
says, "I want a good outcome." But no matter how much you
want to manage the situation, it's largely out of your hands.
Worry will only serve to prove you aren't up to the task. Even
worse, worry is sinister, because you're declaring, "God isn't
big enough to manage this difficulty."

Think about how absurd that is. God, who made the sun,
moon, stars, and this planet we live on; God, who created
and designed human beings, plants, and animals; God, who
ensures that needs are met, seasons begin and end, and the
sun will rise each morning, wants to help you. Does this
sound like a God who can't handle your worst-case scenario?

This is a God who never worries and asks you to bring your worries to Him so He can properly handle them. The antidote to worry is not telling yourself you shouldn't worry—it's prayer. Use this God conversation to remind yourself of God's goodness. Prayers unfurl the God map to show how He has been faithful in the past and help you remember that, more than anyone you know, God knows where He's going, even when you have no idea where to go or what to do.

Worry doesn't need to define your response to the things that concern you. It can be a reminder to pray and get rid of the worry and replace it with a time of worship. Understand that God is bigger than any concern you have, stronger than anything that makes you anxious, and so wonderful that worry seems a pretty useless reaction.

I follow You, and You're my Father. You know how to handle the things that leave me dazed and confused. In moments when worry shows up, help me to remember that is the exact time that coming to You makes the most sense. When worry brings an infestation to my life, be my worry exterminator.

That's Some Kinda Hope

Let your hope make you glad. Be patient in
time of trouble and never stop praying.
ROMANS 12:12 CEV

When you read the word *hope* in the Bible, it has a different meaning than the way it's most often used today. When you hear someone say they hope things get better, they're saying that *better* would be a great outcome, but it might not happen. When they hope they get a better job, they might also be thinking, *That'll be the day*. Hope is thought of as something like wishing upon a star or imagining a best-case scenario while secretly chewing yourself out for such big dreams. Biblical hope doesn't look like that. *Not even a little.*

The reason God's hope can make you glad is that it has nothing to do with wishes or iffy outcomes. Hope is believing beyond a doubt that what God has said will actually happen. His love will be for all people, His forgiveness is available to all, and His rescue plan leaves no one out. Hope believes that no matter what happens today, tomorrow, or next week, God will be there, and His ultimate decision will be right. Hope looks forward to a forever home with God, it conquers the idea that God has abandoned His family, and it looks forward to answered prayer.

Hope requires patience, because what God has promised

doesn't come with a known delivery date. Just because you don't see His answer today doesn't mean it's not going to be answered. He might say no, and He will have a very good reason for doing so, but this hope believes God can do what no one on earth can without Him.

God's answer will not be based on any trends, the depth of your desire for a positive answer, or a feeling that somehow He owes you something. No. His answers are always based on what you actually need to become the man He wants you to be. If what you ask for won't help make that possible, then the request may be denied. But God loves to give good gifts to His family; so unless your request derails His progress in your life, He may say yes, especially if what you request is also something that helps others.

Plant the seed of hope deep inside, God. May my trust in You also give me the wisdom to believe that my future is assured in Your hands. Give me patience as I wait, confident that what You start You also finish. Take my anxiety, stress, and worry. I don't need them when hope finds a home.

Started Here, Finished There

I am sure that God Who began the good work
in you will keep on working in you until
the day Jesus Christ comes again.
PHILIPPIANS 1:6 NLV

God did not leave you with fortune cookies and a book of riddles while instructing you to figure Him out. He offers practical wisdom that will help guide you in your daily journey with Him. He didn't make it hard to know Him, but you do have to pay attention to what He's saying. His way of doing things looks different from the way most people do things. If you think His way has to connect with the way you have learned to do things, then you will always have a struggle.

Get to know God and learn what's important to Him. His wisdom is different from that of the wisest of men. His plan is different from your highest goals. You may be tempted to try to make God fit your preferences, but He never works that way. If you really want to know God, then you should give up trying to remake Him in your image. Learn who He is through what He reveals in His Word.

What may seem like a hardship to you may be God's best gift. His blessing comes in offering rescue and then transforming your old life with all your preconceived notions of how things work. He asks you to reject what you think in favor of what He says. If He's an author, then He doesn't set you aside like a story He has no intention of finishing. If He's an artist, then He keeps painting so the details of your life are clean, clear, and visible. If He's a friend, then He keeps passing along good instructions and helps you understand what He means. He's an author, He's an artist, and He's your friend.

God will keep transforming you until He comes back for you. When that happens, you will receive a new body and you will understand what He needed you to know. You will finally be that new creation He started here—and finished there.

Don't get frustrated. Be patient. God hasn't given up on you, and He continues to work behind the scenes to move from where you are to a place much closer, so you can understand who He is. He has always believed you're worth it.

I sometimes wonder if I'll always let You down, Father. You remind me that You will never fail me. When I'm unfaithful, You keep faithfully working to pull me close so I can keep learning, keep growing, and keep following You.

DAY 30
Forever Faithful

*Know therefore that the LORD your God is God;
he is the faithful God, keeping his covenant of
love to a thousand generations of those who
love him and keep his commandments.*

DEUTERONOMY 7:9 NIV

Above all, beyond any, and with no one who can compete, there's God. He stands with no peer, no equal, and determines truth. His commands are right, just, and unchanging. He is worthy of your holy fear and respect.

One primary reason to respect God is that if you kept track of every instance when you broke a God rule, you would have to consider that infraction as unfaithfulness. The word *unfaithful* has never described God. Not even once. Respect the God who will not leave and never abandons.

God knows you can't be faithful, but there are two things you should know. The first is that He'll always be faithful. He doesn't retaliate by being unfaithful just to show you what that's like. The second is that He never once said that His laws did not need to be followed. He asked for obedience and expects obedience, but He forgives when you disobey. That last one is part of His forever faithfulness.

God has always loved people. That's never changed. Sometimes people show love to God, and it's to those people that

God shows great faithfulness; and because of those who love Him, He shares His faithfulness with the rest of mankind. The reason for God's faithfulness is that He doesn't want anyone to live life apart from Him—now or in the future. He patiently waits for the unconvinced, skeptical, and rejecting. He continues to offer rescue while people demand other options. He reaches out while some slap His hand away in protest. And still He remains faithful.

When you combine your story with God's, you have everything you need to be a witness in the public trials of God that take place in schools, coffee shops, and businesses. You don't have to provide conclusive proof; you just need to share what God has done for you. It's how you add faithfulness to your story. Some will listen.

Find joy in God's faithful story, grip tightly the truth that He offers stability in an unstable world, and know that His promises are just as faithful, true, and fulfilled.

I can't promise perfection, God, but You can. I can't promise faithfulness, but You do. I can't promise that I'll always be trustworthy, but You are. Help me rely on Your faithfulness while You work to transform my heart and redirect my story.

Good Intentions or Great Strength

Young men will fall in exhaustion. But those who trust in the LORD will find new strength. They will soar high on wings like eagles. They will run and not grow weary. They will walk and not faint.

ISAIAH 40:30–31 NLT

Someone once said, "My get up and go got up and went." This saying essentially means that you don't have the energy or motivation to do what you need to do. It happens to all of us when we just can't seem to muster the courage to keep on task.

It could be a project you promised your family you'd get done; it might be the lawn or a project at work. You may have had good intentions, but somehow you just can't find the strength to do what needs to be done. Other people might not understand it and even suggest you just shake it off and keep going. You might be convinced that option is impossible.

When it comes to your spiritual life, God offers the inner strength to do what you're convinced you can't. He offers the courage to accept His help. Your work ethic or intentions are less important than God's ability to recharge your spiritual batteries. He makes you strong, refreshes you, allows you to soar, to run without weariness, and walk without fainting.

God does that. He resets things, charges what needs to be charged, and supplies strength in your weak moments.

Temptation often comes in weak moments, leading to compromise. You might choose to adopt a "who cares" attitude and do what you know you shouldn't because weakness came and you refused to wait on God to answer your prayer to replace your weakness with His strength. You became like the young men in today's verses—you fell in exhaustion. When that happens, you'll often choose to stay down longer than you should, hide when you should want to be found, and choose to lie when you should seek forgiveness.

*I want to be revived, renewed, and refreshed Father.
I want to walk and soar with fresh strength. I want to
live with improved courage. You've offered Your strength,
and I accept Your gift. Help me live beyond good intentions
and refuse to live in weak moments without asking
You for strength that I'll never have on my own.*

Moses' Motivational Moment

God is my strength, God is my song, and, yes!
God is my salvation. This is the kind of God I have
and I'm telling the world! This is the God of my
father—I'm spreading the news far and wide!
EXODUS 15:2 MSG

You've probably had experiences where something good happened and there's no way you could explain it other than to remember that God is good and He cares about you. It could be an unexpected financial gift that paid a bill that was due, a meal paid for by someone ahead of you in the drive-through, or an answer to prayer that could not be explained in any other way but God.

Maybe you've found yourself in a Moses motivational moment. You see, Moses had seen God rescue the people from Egypt and orchestrate an escape route through the Red Sea. That doesn't happen on its own. The verse you read at the top of the page is Moses' response to God's goodness.

You might remember that Moses didn't think He was the right guy for the job of national deliverer, yet God gave him everything he needed to confront Pharaoh. He thought he was too old and not a very good speaker, and maybe he even felt a little too introverted for the task. Yet God made Moses into a leader. He invited Moses to follow and then made the way clear. And when God did that, Moses declared that God was strength, song, and salvation.

Strength—God did what Moses knew he could not.

Song—Only God is worthy of all our praise.

Salvation—God rescues when rescue seems like an impossible dream.

Whenever God sends fresh strength, it is cause for a celebration. Weakness can be overwhelming, debilitating, and frustrating, yet God can turn the scenario on its head and supply an answer that's much more powerful than any individual's weakness.

Tell the world, spread the news, make God famous. Be a witness, share your story, give credit to the One who strengthens. Sing praise, discover worship, and remember God's faithfulness. When God does what He does for you, these are just some of the things you can offer to show your gratitude.

I'm given good gifts every day, God. You keep me from harm and show me where I should plant my next footstep. You offer light, comfort, and friendship. You lead, and when I follow, You take me through the wilderness and into a place of safety. You're my strength when I'm weak. You're my hope when I doubt. You love me when I'm not sure I'm worth it.

DAY 33
Choose God Strength

You are tempted in the same way that everyone else is tempted.
But God can be trusted not to let you be tempted too much,
and he will show you how to escape from your temptations.
1 CORINTHIANS 10:13 CEV

You might believe no one has been tempted like you've been tempted. Your world is a struggle because there are times when you do what you don't want to do, shouldn't do, and God said not to do. Breaking God laws can seem like it's some sort of competitive sport and you're a winner at losing. But God's Word says that you're tempted in the same way as everyone else.

There's no difference between you and someone else. *None.* At least when it comes to temptation. Why? God's Word is a playbook that Satan uses. He knows what God's Word says more than you do. He knows what God wants you to do, and all Satan wants to do is make sure you break as many God rules as he can tempt you to break. He wants you to always be in a place where you require forgiveness. And if he can get you to fail enough, you might just give up on the idea of obedience altogether. If you've been in this place, then you need to know there is God strength to keep God rules.

Here's something to keep in mind: You're tempted in the same way everyone else is tempted, but you can accept

God's help—not everyone will do that. You can stay weak or you can accept His strength—not everyone will ask. You can become cynical and believe there is no way to keep the God rules—you will miss God's escape plan.

There's a way out, and you can take it. There's help, and you can take it. There's hope, so hold on.

You're never forced to face temptation alone. You don't have to make decisions that break God rules without consulting the Rule Maker and getting His input and wisdom. You're never encouraged to stand without His protection.

Discover compassion, knowing that as hard as temptation is for you, it's the same for every person in every town in every country on this planet. Temptation can pull you away from God or it can cause you to run to Him for the strength and help you need.

I've stood guilty far too often, Father. I have to admit that I don't think about inviting You to my struggle before I break Your rules. Give me Your strength to face my battles. That strength gives me the best chance to leave the temptation with the choice to obey.

DAY 34
A Joy Received

He answered me, "I am all you need. I give you My loving-favor. My power works best in weak people." I am happy to be weak and have troubles so I can have Christ's power in me. I receive joy when I am weak. I receive joy when people talk against me and make it hard for me and try to hurt me and make trouble for me. I receive joy when all these things come to me because of Christ. For when I am weak, then I am strong.
2 CORINTHIANS 12:9–10 NLV

No one wants to be seen as weak, but at certain moments in your life, whatever strength you could find hidden away in your life came up short. You crunch the numbers, and the ledger proves weakness no matter how many times you recalculate. You don't want to appear incapable, but there are times when you are incapable. You don't want to appear needy, but sometimes that's just what you are. God knows this. He has the strength you need. Your weakness might just be the best reason to rejoice.

Rejoice *when?* The apostle Paul gave three examples.

When I am weak. That's when God's strength shows up.

When people talk against me. God reminds you that you belong to Him and He'll never stop loving you.

When people make trouble for me. This gives God the opportunity to step in and be your problem solver.

Jesus told Paul (and He says the same thing to you), "I am all you need." When you see your resolve, strength, and perspective weaken, watch God's strength show up. He has always been able to do more than you can on your strongest day.

Recognize what you can't do, and be okay with the deficit, because the God with unlimited resources can use everything He has and can do—for you. Recognize your weakness, and allow God an all-access pass to do the remarkable in your circumstances.

You don't have to be like a four-year-old boy who puffs out his chest and says, "See, Daddy, I'm strong and I can help you." Be that same four-year-old boy who knows what it's like to be hurt and also knows that when Daddy shows up, everything is gonna be all right.

If you didn't have a perfect dad, don't worry. You don't need a bad example to know that God's example is remarkably perfect.

I can have joy in weakness, Father. Trying to be strong without You just delays Your intervention. I want to remember that my weakness isn't seen as a negative by You; it's simply the easiest way for me to say I need Your help.

Unpleasant Field Trips

Even though I walk through the darkest valley,
I will fear no evil, for you are with me.
PSALM 23:4 NIV

You've faced hard stuff, and if by some miracle you haven't, then you know someone who has. It's hard to watch, hard to live through, and hard to consider. You don't wish difficulty for yourself, and you don't want others to face it either. But you will—and they have.

Today's verse makes one thing very clear—trouble will come. It doesn't say, "Even though I may walk." It doesn't say, "Even when other people walk." It doesn't even say, "I've heard that there are some people who walk." Dark valleys come. They're intimidating.

You can gaze from your spiritual mountaintop and know that there is something worth the effort on the other side of the valley; but it will, in fact, mean getting through the valley. From this vantage point, there's light, blue sky, and a pleasant breeze. But in the valley, the shadows lengthen, the vision dims, and worry terrifies. You might get a little claustrophobic as everything seems to close in. This valley is the last place you want to be, but here you are. The only way through is forward. Just remember that you're not alone. You walk with One who is not afraid of the dark, not intimidated by fear, and not the least bit worried.

These dark valleys (some Bible versions read "valley of death") may not be a literal place as much as a life condition. Things like job loss, health issues, or relationship upheaval place you in a valley that's not sunny, pleasant, or desirable. It's a part of life you want to skip, fast-forward through, or get a parental note so you can miss that day, week, month, or year in God's school. But you can't, so just know that your Instructor is with you every moment of this less-than-inviting field trip.

He can lead, He will guide, and His voice comforts you when you're certain that your next step could lead to ruin or regret. Don't walk without Him, don't run ahead, and don't stay behind. This is the place where God's faithfulness gets very personal, His love visible, and from which His care will lead you out.

You know I would rather avoid the unexpected, Father. I like to prepare for what I face, but maybe it's better knowing that You've already done that for me. Give me the courage to follow You when I find myself in unpleasant valleys. When You're with me, I don't need to be afraid of any kind of darkness.

Extra! Extra! Read All about It!

Have you never heard? Have you never understood?
The LORD is the everlasting God, the Creator of all
the earth. He never grows weak or weary. No one
can measure the depths of his understanding.
ISAIAH 40:28 NLT

You can almost imagine the prophet Isaiah as the first corner newspaper salesman. Instead of "Extra! Extra! Read all about it!" He said, "Have you never heard? Have you never understood?" Isaiah was in possession of good news, and he was on the street corner of his time declaring what he knew. And what this prophet knew could change lives. More than shouting headlines, Isaiah drew a crowd and then refused to charge anyone for news that was too good not to share.

If you were on the street that day, you would have gotten an introduction to God. This may have been news to some, but to others it sounded new because they had forgotten God. There were even some who might have thought, *Why are you telling me something I already know?* You see, this introduction was also a reminder. The people had largely walked away from the everlasting Creator, the tireless and wise God.

So this messenger prophet got another chance in this very moment to make his proclamation to those who had never heard, those who had heard and forgotten, and those who knew but had not allowed this good news to make the impact it should.

Have you never heard? Have you never understood? Don't you get it? Does it need to be explained again? *Extra! Extra! Read all about it!* Consider or reconsider this message that is so important that you must use your mind, heart, soul, and spirit to drink it in before you can understand what it means. And when that happens, you must do something about it. The choice to follow is exceptionally wise.

Do you want to be strong? Are you interested in wisdom? Is it possible there's more to life than what you've accepted as normal? *Read God's news.* It's the best thing you'll read today. It can change your life, give you strength, help you understand, and allow you to see that your life has a God-ordained purpose.

Your good news should draw a crowd, God. It should break open hard hearts and closed minds. It should change the path I walk, the people I meet, and the hope I have for the future. You exist without beginning or end, You don't take a vacation, and You know about things that I can only guess about. Keep teaching me Your good news.

DAY 37
The Word Picture Proclamation

*"Don't be afraid. . . . Don't despair. Your GOD is
present among you, a strong Warrior there to save
you. Happy to have you back, he'll calm you with
his love and delight you with his songs."*
ZEPHANIAH 3:17 MSG

While Isaiah called out to a passing crowd and made God introductions, another prophet had a message of his own. Zephaniah had a message with word images that would easily appeal to the crowd. Zephaniah addressed the weak, timid, and anxious, telling them to put aside fear and reject despair. For adventurous people, He referred to God as a strong warrior, capable of complete rescue. He told all the people that God would be happy to have them back. The traitors, the self-righteous, and the doubters in the crowd were not singled out, but they would have understood that a divine reunion was waiting. To the poets and musicians, the message declared that God was a composer and His music would demonstrate love. It would delight all who heard it.

God's message to you doesn't come in only one form. It's a message that reaches who you are—anxious, adventuring, wondering, and artistic. God does not single out one but allows His message to reach people in the exact place where they need to be reached.

Like yesterday's passage from Isaiah, these were people who had once followed but had become seasoned drifters looking for a purpose and plan in anything but God. They needed to notice the message, internalize it, and make it part of their story, but they had to be reached first. They had to know they could return. These messages show God's mercy and grace. He didn't have to spend any time reintroducing Himself. He didn't have to accept their wandering unchallenged. Instead? He used messenger prophets to translate His love into the language of a people who had lived in confusion far too long.

God does the same today. He did the same for you. He's doing something right now that will meet the needs of those who need to know they're not alone and that their lives have meaning, purpose, and significance.

This is a message shared in the Bible, and it's a message you can share with others. God can meet people where they are and invite them to a better future.

You gave me a very specific personality, Father. I came to You with that personality, and You changed my heart by teaching me truth. You can do the same for anyone with any personality. Your words prove that You came for all and desire a friendship with all. Help me make this my big news of the day.

DAY 38
Don't Be a Misinformed Man

God's word is alive and powerful! It is sharper than any
double-edged sword. His word can cut through our spirits
and souls and through our joints and marrow, until it
discovers the desires and thoughts of our hearts.

HEBREWS 4:12 CEV

In a courtroom, two opposing forces attempt to convince a judge or jury that they're telling the correct version of events. At the close of the arguments, a verdict must be made.

Satan has drafted arguments that sound reasonable. In this court of public opinion, he declares that God is dead, His promises broken, and His words antiquated and without any effect on mankind. Some in the gallery will nod their heads and agree with the influence of the argument. In doing so, they stuff down the feeling that they're believing a lie.

Once this master of pride takes his seat, it's time for someone to stand up and declare something altogether different. Today's verse from Hebrews makes the argument. The Bible is God's Word. God's thoughts are contained in this book. Truth hasn't died. Wisdom is active. What God knows exposes spirits, souls, hearts, and minds. This God who has declared His love for mankind also knows everything you want and everything you think.

This is no party trick, and it's not an invasion of your privacy. God made you. He made the rules that govern your life. You can, in fact, think whatever you want, but He still knows what you think. You can make any choice you believe is best, but His truth doesn't change just because your interests have.

And in this unofficial and opinionated court, there will be those who believe Satan's lies. There will be those who leave with that "shadow of a doubt." Some will believe that God is who He says He is, loves the way He declares He does, and can buy people back from Satan's pawn shop.

You could be a spectator in the audience when these kinds of discussions come up, but you likely have evidence to support truth. There's a good God with a good purpose, and His relevance is never determined by the opinions of the misinformed.

You gave me a mind, God, and You gave me a mouth. Let me use these gifts to declare what I know to be true. Like Isaiah and Zephaniah, let me say that You're God, You're good, and You can bring life—even to people who believe You're dead. Help me not to be afraid of human opinions. Help me share truth, because someone somewhere will need to hear it.

Nothing Has Ever Been Too Hard

*"O Lord God! See, You have made the heavens
and the earth by Your great power and by Your
long arm! Nothing is too hard for You!"*

JEREMIAH 32:17 NLV

You just read words of praise from a messenger known as the "weeping prophet." Jeremiah saw the course correction his nation needed, and his sadness was visible. This road would be hard. The people had walked away when God had invited them to walk with Him. Yet this prophet also understood the awesome nature of an invisible God.

People were convinced they were on their own in their struggle, and while they looked to non-gods for answers that provided no help, Jeremiah could proclaim that he was convinced that God made everything in heaven and earth. Jeremiah knew there was no power greater than God and no one was outside His reach. Jeremiah concluded that nothing was outside God's ability to handle.

Are you in the same frame of mind? Maybe you live with lingering doubts. You see evidence of God's work in the lives of people but wonder if He could really be responsible for everything. Maybe you think luck or coincidence plays a role. While you might leave things to chance and circumstance, God doesn't. He knows everything, so He never has to wait to discover how things are going to turn out. Why? He's God.

The impossible is not difficult for God. His promises aren't just possibilities; they are guarantees. Why? He's God.

When you need strength and you read that God's strength is the perfect replacement for your weakness, you might ask yourself, *Why would I hesitate to access the strength of the God who made everything?* Doing everything on your own won't earn above-and-beyond awards or better-than-you badges.

Stand in awe—just like Jeremiah. The God who made everything also controls everything and continues to hold everything together. He loves you enough to offer His help.

I want to take the time to recognize Your wonder, Father. I want to remember that You made everything, and it wasn't even hard for You. And in spite of all You do, You still want to grow a friendship with me. You want me to recognize that You know everything about me and still choose to help me every day that I'm willing to let You help.

DAY 40
Embracing Destruction?

*If you harbor bitter envy and selfish ambition in your hearts,
do not boast about it or deny the truth. Such "wisdom" does
not come down from heaven but is earthly, unspiritual,
demonic. For where you have envy and selfish ambition,
there you find disorder and every evil practice.*

JAMES 3:14–16 NIV

You'll be reading about real wisdom over the next few days, but to recognize wisdom, you need to know that there are times when the word *wisdom* is applied to certain actions that don't fit God's idea of what wisdom should look like. Today's devotional will allow you to compare and contrast real wisdom with what some mislabeled "wisdom."

The three verses you read above paint a picture of the way a business can crumble from within, how relationships suffer when care is replaced by envy and selfishness, and how disorder is the outcome of decisions made when pride is king.

It's not wise to use the things you want as a motivation to destroy someone else. It's not wise to think that you can say you meant no harm when you worked overtime to do something you were pretty certain could destroy someone. That destruction could be their livelihood, life's work, reputation, or family. Instead of feeling badly about your actions or seeking to make things right, you secretly consider your actions an achievement you're proud of.

You've probably entertained this type of destructive wisdom. Rejecting it is always a good call, but when someone doesn't reject this false wisdom and instead embraces destruction, that's a reminder that God can't be blamed for the poor decisions of others. Bad things will happen, and sometimes those things get started because someone thinks they have chosen wisdom when what they've really done is far more sinister—God calls it evil.

If you think the world seems chaotic, then it's not much of a stretch to take God's view of earthly wisdom and see that disorder is always the outcome of accepting this broken bit of selfish "wisdom." It doesn't see other people as worth considering when making any decision. It looks for an outcome it likes and doesn't think it's worth spending too much time considering how it might impact others. It removes empathy of the heart from the decisions of the mind.

I don't want to embrace destruction, God. I want to care about people and allow You to bring success when You think it's the right time. Help me learn more about Your wisdom and want the same for my life.

DAY 41
The Wisdom Contrast

*The wisdom from above is first of all pure. It is also
peace loving, gentle at all times, and willing to yield
to others. It is full of mercy and the fruit of good deeds.
It shows no favoritism and is always sincere.*

JAMES 3:17 NLT

Yesterday you learned that commonly accepted wisdom is simply doing whatever you can to get ahead without worrying about who could be hurt by your actions. This wisdom will even go so far as to do things that will intentionally hurt others if it means a personal goal can be achieved. If you fast-forward one more verse, you gain access to the contrast between this kind of wisdom and God wisdom.

While common wisdom can express itself as evil, God's wisdom will always be pure. When common wisdom is disruptive, God's wisdom seeks peace. When common wisdom is destructive, God's wisdom is gentle. When common wisdom takes control from others, God's wisdom makes others more important. When common wisdom is ruthless, God's wisdom is merciful. When common wisdom rests on the trash heap of wrong choices, God's wisdom can be found growing within the fruit of the good-deed tree. When common wisdom says only some people are important, God's wisdom never plays favorites. When common wisdom says what it needs to say to get what it wants, God's wisdom is sincere and truthful.

This is a pretty powerful list of contrasts, but knowing what true wisdom is not is helpful to understanding what true wisdom is. You hear people describe wisdom as doing what you can do to improve your own position in society. It only includes other people when they can help you achieve what you want to do. If they can't help you, then they're viewed as expendable. These people are only useful as long as they serve a purpose in your plan. This wisdom views people as tools rather than as human beings. As you've read, God's opinion differs dramatically.

God's wisdom includes others; works to achieve mutual goals; and refuses to step on others, crush their dreams, or break their hearts.

Choose God's wisdom, follow His example, and invite others to the experience. They'll need to see what God's wisdom looks like when it's lived out through a guy like you.

I'm amazed that Your wisdom found You thinking of me, Father. My good has been factored into Your wisdom. Help me accept Your wisdom, follow Your advice, and discover that caring about others is always in Your plans. This wisdom is Your expectation for men who follow You. Help me meet Your expectations.

Prayer Asks the Question

If you don't know what you're doing, pray to the
Father. He loves to help. You'll get his help, and won't
be condescended to when you ask for it. Ask boldly,
believingly, without a second thought. People who
"worry their prayers" are like wind-whipped waves.
Don't think you're going to get anything from the Master
that way, adrift at sea, keeping all your options open.
JAMES 1:5–8 MSG

Knowing what to do every minute of the day seems impossible. You want to make good choices, but then you don't make them. You have a plan, but then it doesn't work out. You think you know the answer, but you're proven wrong. It's enough to make a guy think that giving up makes sense.

When you find yourself in this place, you can and should come to God. He won't belittle you and make you feel pathetic for asking. He's not tired of helping you. Never that. He loves to see you actually believe that He can help. His wisdom is strong and steady.

Don't arrive in prayer feeling timid and fearful. God wants you to know that as a Christian you can come to Him like a child comes to their father to ask for something they need. This child is bold and never doubts for a minute that their dad can help. Children believe that adults in their life can set things right. In the real world, that's not always possible, but there is God.

He helps the hurting, lonely, and sad. He stands with the crushed, broken, and impatient. He lifts up the humble, meek, and weak. And God wants you to be so comfortable in His presence that you'll pray bold prayers and believe He can answer. Don't demand that God do anything more than what He knows is best for you; but be specific about what you think you need, and allow God to change your mind whenever He needs to.

Your prayers will never require you to think trusting God is just one of many different options. Don't walk into prayer with an "It can't hurt" mentality.

God is the answer. Prayer asks the question. The only option you need is the one thing you can do right now. *Pray.*

I can be confused, God. My mind will allow my mouth to say words it isn't even thinking. Help me focus on the questions that only You can answer. I don't want to be afraid, and I don't want to seek a second opinion. Please answer and help me accept what You know will be the best for me.

A Man of Few Words

It makes a lot of sense to be a person of few words and to
stay calm. Even fools seem smart when they are quiet.
PROVERBS 17:27–28 CEV

Do you know someone who is easily angered and makes you feel uncomfortable around them? Do you find it easy to share opinions with that person, or do you keep those opinions under lock and key?

God's Word says a lot about wisdom, and this is a very basic and practical bit of advice. If you can limit your word count when words aren't essential, and if you refuse to get angry so that negative words don't fire through the air with the precision of a guided missile, many people will consider you a wise man.

It's true that words can inspire people to do something more, be something better, or try something wonderful. Words can also rip the fabric of emotional trauma that you know nothing about. Your words can move beyond the tear and cause fresh hurt in ancient wounds. You may not mean for anything like that to happen, but it can, it does, and it will. Wisdom learns when to speak, and that may be less often than you think.

If you use your mind more than your mouth, then when you do have something important to say, you'll likely find that people are more willing to listen and consider what you say. It's possible they won't see you as someone who says whatever's on your mind but someone who takes the time to consider many things before you speak. The impact of what you have to say is greater when that happens.

Don't be surprised if the more you think about what you might say helps you conclude more often that whatever you were going to say doesn't need to be said. That's not always the case, and there are times when you need to speak up; but becoming more of an observer than a participant in mindless conversations might just leave you with less regret, more satisfaction, and engaged in the actions of a man God considers wise.

Remove words from my tongue that don't need to be said,
Father. From needless sarcasm to insensitivity, change my
mind and rearrange my words, so that what needs to be said
will be seen as important and what doesn't need to be said
is never heard. Your words show love and invite friendship.
They share truth and invite change. Help me to be like You.

DAY 44
What Few Are Willing to Do

I ask God that you may know what He wants
you to do. I ask God to fill you with the wisdom
and understanding the Holy Spirit gives.
COLOSSIANS 1:9 NLV

You probably have no idea why people do what they do. It can be confusing, frustrating, infuriating. They could choose good but don't. They could choose love but won't. They could choose kindness, but something less noble takes its place. And just when you consider making a social media post railing about someone else's lack of civility, you catch a glimpse in a mirror. If you can believe what you see, you've been one who failed to choose good, left love behind, and failed to show kindness. This reflection surprises you. These are things you could show to other people that would really be meaningful, but it's easier to have good intentions than to actually do what you know God wants you to do.

Pray for others and ask them to pray for you. They can ask God to give you the wisdom you need to do the right thing. They can ask God to help you be brave enough to do what few are willing to do. While some people feel put out for having to put up with others, God might give you enough love not only to be willing but even eager to care for such people. When you want to shout, "Grow up!" when others annoy you, God might remind you that growing is exactly what *you* are doing when you seek His wisdom for dealing with irritating people. When you want to pray, "I don't think I can do this," you might discover that God says, "I know; let Me help."

You don't need to fake it to make it. You just need to obey. You can even admit it's hard and that sometimes you'd rather give up. But giving up is something you don't have to do. Let God help you by fueling your actions with wise words and a profound understanding of how He does things and why. His perspective will change yours.

*Give me Your heart so I can feel how You feel about people,
God. Give me Your eyes so I can see a clarity in the way
people can be redeemed. Give me a hope that recognizes
that You're waiting for people to come to You. I can either
be someone who helps or someone who stands in the
way. Help me to be the first someone, not the last.*

A Recipe They've Never Tried

Be wise in the way you act toward outsiders;
make the most of every opportunity. Let your
conversation be always full of grace, seasoned with salt,
so that you may know how to answer everyone.
COLOSSIANS 4:5–6 NIV

You may have had a mom or grandma who could cook really well. You couldn't wait to sample some of their creations. They had bottles, bags, and shakers filled with things you'd never heard of, but when all of those things were put together in a bowl, blender, or pan, they made the most amazing food. Some you may be remembering right now.

As the years passed, maybe you learned about things like spices, herbs, and other seasonings. You learned how yeast changes dough and how correct oven temperatures and times result in perfect confections.

You know this because you experienced it first and then learned how to duplicate what you experienced. This is what happens in the life of a Christian. You can experience God's love first, accept His offer of rescue, then sample God's goodness and discover it's very good.

When you take the time to learn more about God, you can then share what you're learning with others who haven't experienced God's love, accepted His rescue, or acknowledged

His goodness. This is a good recipe that blends the perfect ingredients to result in an impressive taste experience.

So when anyone asks about the difference between what they've experienced and what they see in you, just remember you're part of a living recipe they've never tried.

The words you use can describe the recipe, give it a glowing review, and encourage people to sample the end result, but you don't get to force anyone to make a choice. They could choose not to because they seem certain it's not for them, they don't like some of the ingredients, or they think the recipe is only for certain people. You'll need wisdom to know how to use your words and when to stop using them. Remember: you're adding seasoning—you will never be the entire recipe.

You can be part of God's plan to extend rescue to others. You *should* be part of that plan, but you need to remember that God is the one who actually does the rescuing. *That's wisdom.*

Give me the wisdom to remember that Your plan includes me, Father, but that Your plan has never said that I have to be the one to do what only You can do. I want to participate in sharing Your recipe for salvation, but help me remember that I must never try to take Your place.

DAY 46
The Rejected—The Rejecter

There is no longer Jew or Gentile, slave or free, male and female. For you are all one in Christ Jesus.
GALATIANS 3:28 NLT

What is prejudice? Is it just a skin tone issue, or does it go further? Prejudice is anything that is used to keep someone out, away from, or beyond what you're doing. It refuses to include some people. It's a feeling that somehow some people have greater worth than other people. Some world leaders have even gone so far as to commit genocide (the killing of people of a certain culture). The apostle Paul gave God's perspective on prejudice in today's verse.

You won't find a certain preference for people God accepts in this verse. You don't have to fill out an application to find out if you measure up. The true test is agreeing that everyone sins and therefore everyone needs God to rescue them. John 3 describes God's love as something that leaves no one out. *No one.* The verse above says that cultures are irrelevant and socioeconomic status doesn't count. God considers males and females equal, and the end result should be a family who works together to get His work done. God looks at people and sees humans who need Him. Don't accept the lie that says people need to be broken down into classes like *sinner* and *worse sinner*, *acceptable* and *unacceptable*.

That's much easier than being someone who accepts others. Why is that? Humans want to know where they fit, so they compare themselves with people around them. Those who are different might make you uncomfortable, and they might not seem like someone you could be friends with. Yet at their core, they're individuals made in God's image who need rescuing. Maybe they've already been rescued. What prevents you from accepting them?

Your dislike for another person is more likely to change you than it is to change them. Any hatred you feel is a tool used to change you—but never in a good way.

Being rejected is no fun. Being the rejecter means you disagree with God. Quick note: *God's right.*

I may have grown up believing some people were better than others, God. You say that Your love came for all and You'll rescue anyone who asks. When what I've thought disagrees with what You've said, help change my mind. Help change my heart. Help me love those You love. I know this will take me out of my comfort zone, so I'll also need Your help making this move toward new understanding.

Your "Reaching Out" Adventure

*Even though I am free of the demands and expectations of
everyone, I have voluntarily become a servant to any and all
in order to reach a wide range of people: religious, nonreligious,
meticulous moralists, loose-living immoralists, the defeated, the
demoralized—whoever. I didn't take on their way of life. I kept
my bearings in Christ—but I entered their world and tried
to experience things from their point of view. I've become just
about every sort of servant there is in my attempts to lead those I
meet into a God-saved life. I did all this because of the Message.
I didn't just want to talk about it; I wanted to be in on it!*

1 CORINTHIANS 9:19–23 MSG

If you want the adventure of a lifetime, then reread today's
passage. The only one you answer to is God, and He said to
love people. So your adventure is reaching out and loving
people—*all people* (read the first few lines above for examples).

This passage was written from the perspective of the
apostle Paul. He wasn't saying that you should find people
who don't love God and then act like them. He was saying to
bring God's love with you into others' lives because it has the
power to change them. Paul concluded, "I didn't take on their
way of life. I kept my bearings in Christ—but I entered their
world and tried to experience things from their point of view."

That can be a hard thing to do. If you tried to be like

them in order to be accepted by them, or on the flip side, you verbally punished them for their way of life, in both instances you would make it nearly impossible for them to accept your message. When you act like them, they don't see any need to change. When you tell them how wrong they are, they don't see you as having information they don't already suspect. Spend time telling anyone you meet about the goodness of God. Let the Holy Spirit stand as the subject matter expert. Let His example change a life.

The result of what you do could be a God-saved life, but not if you try to be just like them and not if you try to be their judge. Build relationships by caring for others and sharing good news.

You don't live in a box, Father. You're the best example of an adventurer I know. There's no place You won't go to reach out to someone lost and in need of rescue. Yet I can be one who hides within my own four walls and keeps away from those who need You. Help me to be more like You.

Chronically Short–Sighted

Don't love the world or anything that belongs to the world. If you love the world, you cannot love the Father. Our foolish pride comes from this world, and so do our selfish desires and our desire to have everything we see. None of this comes from the Father.
1 JOHN 2:15–16 CEV

The desire for things can be overwhelming. You probably don't need examples of things you'd love to own. You've been to a showroom, you've shopped online, and you've probably even looked through things other people own and no longer want. You've had your eye on something. You want what you don't have. You might even dream about something you want, pray for it, or take another job to pay for it.

Loving the here and now (earth) instead of the then and there (heaven) is a short-sighted perspective that offers you only something temporary. It has an expiration date. This obsession with your present condition keeps you from looking at God's bigger picture. If His greatest command is to love—*and it is*—then relationships will always be more important than anything you can own temporarily. In fact, relationships are priceless, but material things fall apart and are often declared trash by a new generation.

Stories are often told of people who kept everything they

had even a small attachment to. When they passed, their families were left to deal with things they had little attachment to. The result is often dumpsters filled and refilled with someone's sentimental treasures that hold no value to anyone else. Yet the one who owned them kept these things closer than most people. The sad end result is the decreased value of relationships for the rust and dust of things.

God made people to love and things to enjoy. Don't give in to the temptation to love stuff instead. Almost anything you buy today will not have the same value in a year or two. This is true for those who observe what you own and for yourself. It won't be long before you determine that item that was a must-have needs to be replaced.

People, however, last forever. They're important to God, and they can impact both their present and future. Remember that God said the world would one day be destroyed, but you will live forever, either on the new earth or in hell. God's creation was less important to Him than you are.

Help me remember that people will always be more important than things I can own, God. Help me build relationships and be content to enjoy the things I already have. I don't want to be obsessed with all things new and shiny, but I do want to follow You and love Your family.

DAY 49
Content—Remarkably

I have learned to be happy with whatever I have.
I know how to get along with little and how to live when
I have much. I have learned the secret of being happy at
all times. If I am full of food and have all I need, I am
happy. If I am hungry and need more, I am happy. I can
do all things because Christ gives me the strength.

PHILIPPIANS 4:11–13 NLV

If you never own more than you have right now, would it be enough? Would you complain? Would things seem unfair? Would you blame God?

The apostle Paul seemed to have a feast or famine life. There were times when he had everything he needed and other times that were lean and difficult. Paul seemed to suggest there is a learning curve. Going from plenty to plenty of nothing can be difficult.

Paul said he had times when food was hard to find and he felt hungry. But he reached a point in his adventure with God where he was satisfied (content, happy) whether he was full or running on empty. He realized that his hope in God meant that he knew God still loved him and looked out for him; and no matter how bad things got, Paul knew he would one day see God face-to-face. He would never be hungry again. The lean days would be over, the feast days would never end.

The God of this future gives His strength on the leanest of days, helps when help is most needed, and promises never to abandon His own. Knowing this can leave a person remarkably content.

It's not especially hard to become discontent. You might dream of an improved future. When things don't go your way, you might feel betrayed by a God you thought would help you reach your dreams. On the other hand, contentment wants God's dream and is patient while it waits for all things to work for good.

Contentment holds on for the better day to come and refuses to demand improvement to a less-than-ideal today. Contentment might pray for that relief but accepts God's answer—yes, no, or wait.

My heart can long for more when it should long for You, Father. It can get distracted when it sees others with plenty. It can yearn to trust things instead of You. Paul lived during lean times and experienced plenty. Yet he thought there was no difference between the two when it came to how good You are. I want to view my circumstances that way. I want to be content.

DAY 50
Pocket of God's Peace

Trust in the Lord and do good; dwell in the land
and enjoy safe pasture. Take delight in the Lord,
and he will give you the desires of your heart.
Commit your way to the Lord; trust in him.

Psalm 37:3–5 niv

Have you lived in the pocket of God's peace? It's not just a great place to visit; it can be your home. This isn't a place where you hide from the world; it's simply the best place to experience a peace you can't understand because it's somehow more powerful than the struggles you face.

This pocket is available when you line up your priorities with God's. You'll make a commitment to alter your way of doing things when it conflicts with God's way. You'll trust in God when it would be easier to ignore His instructions.

This is a place of wisdom. It offers a home to contentment. It welcomes regular God conversations when you read His words and pray. It may seem difficult because this decision might make it hard to spend time with old thoughts, old choices, and old habits. But you'll find new choices on your way to a future filled with new hope.

The pocket of God's peace is a deep sigh of satisfaction. It's knowing for certain that you'll never make a better decision than to pay attention to where God is moving and go there. This special place is a gift. You can't get there on your own, and you're okay with not knowing because you know the Giver of good gifts and you've learned to say yes when He offers new gifts.

You could settle for less, a substitute might catch your attention, or you could even live with the fear of what it might mean to rely fully on God. The pocket of God's peace is not a place where trouble can't reach you, but it is a place where God patiently walks with you in the safety of His protection.

And when the things that delight your soul are the same as the things that delight God's heart, you get to live with the knowledge that God wants to answer positively those prayers that are in agreement with what He wants.

Live in the pocket of God's peace. There's no better place to be.

I get to walk with You, God. You promise to walk with me. You also ask me to learn from You so that when I follow, You get to lead someone who is willing and not someone who struggles to recall that there's a path where You want me to walk. Help me live comfortably in the pocket of Your peace.

Peace in Conflict

You will keep in perfect peace all who trust in
you, all whose thoughts are fixed on you!
Isaiah 26:3 nlt

How important would it be to you to live in a place of peace? Sounds inviting, doesn't it? God offers one kind of peace, but there is another, earthly, kind of peace as well. Most people think of peace as the absence of conflict; but a better way to understand peace is as resting in the confidence that God is in control even when you find yourself living in the midst of chaos.

When you think that God means you will never experience chaos when He delivers peace, then you may not be taking into account the truth that you don't live in a perfect world. Other people may be very intentional about creating drama, stirring up controversy, opposing truth, and making life hard for others. If God meant you would have no conflict, then He would need to make all decisions for all people in all places, but the truth is people choose to follow God or go as far the opposite way as they can. This means that even if there were only two people on earth and only one follows God, then there would still be conflict between those two people.

It can be easy to read a verse like the one at the start of today's reading and conclude that God wants to make your life easy with no conflict. But this kind of peace is reserved for heaven.

Keep your focus on God, and allow Him to do something inside you that prevents apprehension when chaos arrives. God has never promised a Christian life without struggle, but He did promise to go through the struggle with you. He did promise to take care of you in the middle of another promise—to stay in control of things. He also promised to love you.

A popular song says that God's peace flows like a river. It covers a lot of ground, it overflows its banks, it covers every part of an anxious life you can leave behind. Ask for that kind of peace.

If I had my way, there would be no conflict, Father.
When people get to choose their response, there will always
be conflict. Help me understand that Your peace for Your
family exists in the middle of conflict and trouble. It doesn't
need to be affected by struggle. Help me learn to trust You
enough to allow peace to replace the worry I sometimes
feel. Keep my eyes on You rather than on the struggle.

How Much Is Enough?

"Give me enough food to live on, neither too much
nor too little. If I'm too full, I might get independent,
saying, 'God? Who needs him?' If I'm poor, I might
steal and dishonor the name of my God."

Proverbs 30:8–9 msg

Some people go to extremes in their friendship with God. Some believe that they should give everything away and live from meal to meal, never quite knowing where that will come from. Others ask God for lots of money to buy lots of things to fill lots of wants. The author of today's proverb suggests a Goldilocks approach to the requests you make from God. Not too much, not too little, but the just right amount (and God gets to decide what that is for you).

You see, there can be a conflict of Christian character when wanting too little or too much. When you don't have enough, you can become desperate and do things you wouldn't normally do (like stealing). If you have too much, you can't seem to hear the cries of the desperate needing help.

God gave plenty of examples of how people who had more could share with people who had less. This kind of intentional act of giving means something. It doesn't matter if you have little or much because the end result is still the need to trust God to take care of you. The poor might believe

God won't help, and the rich think they gained their wealth on their own. The writer of this proverb was convinced that if God could simply provide what he actually needed, then he wouldn't need to be desperate and he wouldn't have to be greedy. That would seem to lead to peace and satisfaction, knowing that God provides.

You need God. He knows it, and you suspect it. It's strange that money and things you can buy with it seem to be things that can separate you from trusting Him. Even money printed in the United States can serve as a reminder to trust in God. That's good advice.

You might give me the skills to do a job, God. Thank You. You might bring someone to help. I'm grateful. You might make me wait just a little bit longer. Teach me to be patient. Give me what I need. No more. No less. Help me to be content with Your answer and to trust Your wisdom. I want Your just-right answer to the problems I face. Help me believe that what You send is what I've needed all along. Help me discover gratitude when You answer.

DAY 53
Waiting for Your Arrival

"Don't store up treasures on earth! Moths and rust can destroy
them, and thieves can break in and steal them. Instead, store
up your treasures in heaven, where moths and rust cannot
destroy them, and thieves cannot break in and steal them.
Your heart will always be where your treasure is."
MATTHEW 6:19–21 CEV

You might have bank accounts, money market accounts, and individual retirement accounts. You've planned for your future and sacrificed now for things you might need later. God tells us to count the costs today because it's just the right kind of policy when it comes to business.

There's a problem though. When your future only extends to the rest of your physical life, then you haven't come close to planning far enough ahead. The most important part of your existence will be after you die. You can't take any of the financial accounts with you when you enter heaven, but you can prepare now for your life there.

The things you think are important now won't last. Even if they're still in working condition when you die, they're still used, still worth less than you paid for them, and they can still be destroyed. When you choose to do what God asks, there are rewards that will be waiting when you begin your forever life with God in heaven.

It's true that you may not see those rewards in this lifetime, but that doesn't mean that they aren't yours—you just need to wait to receive them. Because they aren't delivered now, there are a lot of people who choose not to do what God asks. They don't see any immediate benefits. This thinking generally comes from a risk and reward concept. You take a risk and do something adventurous, and you see the reward for taking that risk. To obey God might mean you don't see the ultimate reward until you move from earth to heaven. Some just don't want to wait that long. That's why today's verses exist. Nothing you own here will mean much there. What you get there will be better than anything you've experienced here. Obey and be patient. Good things lie ahead.

You know I can be impatient, Father. Teach me that the best things in life aren't things and that the best future is not having more money but having more of You. Teach me to wait when I'd rather not, follow when I'd rather sit, and go when I'd rather stay. Show me where to go. Help me want to go where You lead. I look forward to seeing You when I come home.

DAY 54
Love or Money

The love of money is the beginning of all kinds of sin.
Some people have turned from the faith because of their love for
money. They have made much pain for themselves because of this.
But you, man of God, turn away from all these sinful things.
Work at being right with God. Live a God-like life. Have
faith and love. Be willing to wait. Have a kind heart.
1 TIMOTHY 6:10–11 NLV

You've probably heard that the Bible doesn't say money is evil, rather that money is the root of all evil. It can start you on the road to sinful choices. Some people reject God because money becomes more important.

Money is a tool. It helps you do things you normally can't do without it. But this tool also accesses things that may not be good for you. God wants you to stop loving money before needing to endure a course correction. And because guys generally like a multistep plan of action to get from point A to point B, let's check out God's list.

Step 1: *Turn away from all these sinful things.* You start with a choice, and it's a choice you will need to continually make.

Step 2: *Work at being right with God.* Take your relationship with Him seriously and follow Him faithfully.

Step 3: *Live a Christlike life.* He's your example. Make the choice you made in step 1 each day to reflect on what you're learning.

Step 4: *Have faith and love.* Trust God and show compassion to others.

Step 5: *Be willing to wait.* Be patient. Endure hard days. Expect delays.

Step 6: *Have a kind heart.* There's never a need to respond with rudeness. Even when someone else is rude, you don't have to respond that way. This, too, is a choice.

All of these things can be accomplished with or without money. They can all be accomplished with God's help.

Accomplish. With God.

*You want my life to be bigger than money, God.
You want my choices to be more important than things.
You want my heart to long for You and not for things
obtained with cash. Teach me self-control and the
wisdom that comes with waiting for Your best.*

Keep Rejoicing

*The stone the builders rejected has become the cornerstone; the
LORD has done this, and it is marvelous in our eyes. The LORD
has done it this very day; let us rejoice today and be glad.*

PSALM 118:22–24 NIV

The apostle Paul wrote that you should start the day rejoicing
and then keep rejoicing, just as you should love then keep
loving, stand and keep standing, forgive and keep forgiving.
The Bible is filled with things you can begin doing today and
then keep doing.

The book of Psalms also encourages you to rejoice. In
some Bible translations, you'll read something like "This is
the day the LORD has made. We will rejoice and be glad in it"
(v. 24 NLT). Praise songs have been written about this verse,
but many people have no idea why they are being asked to
rejoice. The two verses before the rejoicing part tell why you
should rejoice—why you still can.

The act of rejoicing means you're convinced there's something important enough to recognize and then to stand in
awe of something that's amazing. You rejoice when your favorite team makes it to the championship game. You rejoice
when your son or daughter comes home with an impressive
report card. You rejoice when you receive an unexpected
raise. See? Reasons to rejoice. But none are God's primary
reason to rejoice.

This psalm is prophetic. The writer foretold something that would happen in the future. The psalmist was talking about the arrival of Jesus centuries before Jesus was born.

The day that Jesus brought rescue was *the day* God had planned long before Jesus was born, and it was this day that the psalmist declared he would rejoice in long before it happened. That's the day the disciples found reason to rejoice, for they had put their trust in the rejected cornerstone (Jesus). It's the day you can rejoice in too, because God's rescue plan is still available today.

Because Jesus came, you need never stop rejoicing, for the news of the Savior is just as inspiring on this day as it was the moment centuries ago when the ink was drying on the written words of a psalm that told everyone Jesus was on His way.

Your Son, Jesus, was the rejected cornerstone that no one seemed to want, Father. But He was the One who brought rescue to mankind. That's amazing. That's what brings the inspiration for rejoicing. And rejoicing is what I'm doing today and will do forever.

DAY 56
Losing It All

*Even though the fig trees have no blossoms, and there are
no grapes on the vines; even though the olive crop fails,
and the fields lie empty and barren; even though the flocks die
in the fields, and the cattle barns are empty, yet I will rejoice
in the LORD! I will be joyful in the God of my salvation!*
HABAKKUK 3:17–18 NLT

It's possible that people can believe that God promised something He didn't. He said He would bless people but never promised that the blessing would be money or things. He promised abundant life, but He never said life would be easy. In fact, God promised something very unexpected—*trouble* (John 16:33).

A good by-product of experiencing trouble is that you'll see your need for God's help. Without living through trouble, you won't learn patience, endurance, and trust in God. You might believe you can manage life on your own.

Two verses in the Old Testament book of Habakkuk describe struggle through the eyes of a farmer who loved God and followed Him faithfully. This man could claim that if every crop he grew and every animal he raised came to nothing, even this couldn't stop him from finding joy in the God who saves. If every crop failed and the barn was empty, it couldn't stop his mouth from forming praise. The writer was publicly declaring that even in bankruptcy and utter defeat, nothing could diminish the love and gratefulness he had for God.

Could the same be said of you? Could you say, "Even though clients make no purchase and no new customers can be found; even though I am no longer allowed to order new product and my store lies empty and barren; even though I am bankrupt and I experience foreclosure, yet I will rejoice in the Lord! I will be joyful in the God of my salvation!"

Personalizing today's verses may leave you in a panic. No one wants to see financial ruin, but you should be grateful that joy comes from God and that the circumstances you face will never make God less faithful than He has always been.

I'm the most content when I trust You, God. I'm the most joyful when I remember that while You didn't have to rescue me, it was a choice You wanted to make. That's more important than anything I could ever own or any success I might encounter. Keep my heart leaning on You.

DAY 57
Credentials

The very credentials these people are waving around as something special, I'm tearing up and throwing out with the trash—along with everything else I used to take credit for. And why? Because of Christ. Yes, all the things I once thought were so important are gone from my life. Compared to the high privilege of knowing Christ Jesus as my Master, firsthand, everything I once thought I had going for me is insignificant—dog dung. I've dumped it all in the trash so that I could embrace Christ and be embraced by him.

PHILIPPIANS 3:7–8 MSG

Make no mistake, the apostle Paul had credentials. He was among the elite of religious observers. He was known by name and was groomed for leadership. He didn't have to back down to many. Yet he would back down to Jesus. He was used to seeing friends waving their credentials like flags and screeching to be heard among the crowd. They had rivals fighting for rank and begging to be noticed.

Paul left this way of life behind. He stopped taking credit for things God had done. The honor of knowing Jesus was worth more to Paul than the long introductions and even longer résumé.

The apostle began to understand that while God *is* famous, the people he had surrounded himself with *wanted to be* famous. They used God as a tool to gain prestige and power. There came a point when Paul determined that this approach would never please God, for God was looking for people who would serve Him and forge relationships with others. Paul began to see that everything he thought was important was less useful than last week's newspaper at the bottom of a birdcage.

Rejecting the attraction to fame is one of the reasons Paul is remembered. He rejected fame because of a relationship with God. That relationship changed him from a zealot to a servant, a religious snob to a student, and a persecutor of Christians to a missionary.

This was quite a transformation. Paul had been a star for those who were religious but rejected God's Son. He could have had that kind of power and persuasion for the rest of his life. And if that had been his course of action, he would have missed out on the best friendship of his life and the greatest hope for his future. He made his choice. Everyone must.

You tell me who I am, Father. There's no paper that can make me what You've decided I should be. There's no title that's more spectacular than Yours. You're Savior, Redeemer, Forgiver, Lord, and God. Help me to follow You more than my personal ambition.

DAY 58
Be a Resource Manager

God can bless you with everything you need,
and you will always have more than enough
to do all kinds of good things for others.
2 CORINTHIANS 9:8 CEV

If you want to do more for others, be more for those around you, and share more, God can give you more to do selfless work.

God wants you to be a good manager of what He gives. Today's verse suggests that when you wisely and generously steward the resources God provides for you, He will provide additional resources so that you can help others even more.

If you're a parent, you probably don't want to give resources to your children if you know they'll only use those resources to display their bent toward selfishness. You might want them to share some and save some and use the rest wisely for personal needs and wants. Why would God be any different? He provides all the instruction you need for managing the resources He provides, but too often His instruction is overlooked or misunderstood.

God gives so that you can give and cares so that you can care, and His great gift of love is never meant to be kept to yourself. Share what God gives, and don't be surprised if somehow you have a little more to share the next time there's a need. Do you share money? Maybe. Food? Some people need it. Time? It's a gift more precious than money, costs very little, but is often overlooked.

A heart willing to share what God has given is a gift more meaningful than you can imagine. God's gifts are not designed to make you personally rich in resources, but rich in compassion—and this compassion responds by sharing and loving.

When I want to keep what I have, I'm not managing Your resources very well, Father. If being stingy is normal, then I can be very normal. When I have a little, I want to keep a lot. I can believe that giving is something other people do and that I don't have enough to share. But You never ask me to give what I don't have. You ask me to share what I actually have. You say that when I'm faithful with small things, You will trust me with more resources to use to help others.

DAY 59
God's Unexpected Good

Praise the Lord, O my soul. And all that is within me, praise
His holy name. Praise the Lord, O my soul. And forget none of
His acts of kindness. He forgives all my sins. He heals all my
diseases. He saves my life from the grave. He crowns me with
loving-kindness and pity. He fills my years with good things.
PSALM 103:1–5 NLV

Plan your life well, and do all the good you can. That sounds
like a great life motto, but it leaves God out. Being a moral
person is a fine thing—God wants you to have good morals—
but without the Holy Spirit living within you, you will fall
short of what God requires.

King David wrote Psalm 103. He knew that it was much
wiser to praise God than to praise himself. He knew that all
of his goodness came from God and that no matter how hard
he tried, he couldn't be perfect. He was wise to praise the
"Heart Changer" and not himself, the "behavior modifier."
Likewise, when it's up to you to make perfect decisions, you'll
fail. Too many hindrances get in the way of good intentions.

When you get past your personal best choices, you get to
God. When you take His greatness in, you'll likely remember
how kind and forgiving He has been to you, how He healed
you when you were sick, and how He rescued you when things
could have turned out very differently. Filling your life with

good things is what God does, and praise is what you can use to remember those good things.

Go back and read the first sentence again. Doing all the good you can is something that's made easier when you let God help you. He offers opportunities, and you may find resources in unexpected places. God has good things planned for you and for you to do. Look for the things God is doing, and you might be surprised by how easily you can be plugged into that work.

I want to remember Your goodness, Father, and do good things as well. So help me to remember to rely on You to make good choices. You deserve all the praise for any good that comes from me.

DAY 60
God's Footprints

*Blessed is the one who does not walk in step with the wicked
or stand in the way that sinners take or sit in the company of
mockers, but whose delight is in the law of the LORD, and who
meditates on his law day and night. That person is like a tree
planted by streams of water, which yields its fruit in season
and whose leaf does not wither—whatever they do prospers.*

PSALM 1:1–3 NIV

Someone will lead and you will follow. You'll always have an
example to watch even if it's a bad example. This could be a
family member, friend, or even an enemy. You pay attention
to what they do and decide either to follow or reject what
they do. And you might be the example someone else follows.

Leaders may never say they want you to follow, but often
you will. They may be someone with influence, someone you
want to emulate, or someone you dislike so much that you do
what they do without even realizing it because their actions
are what you think about most of the time.

Don't spend time tracking the wicked. Don't stand on the
corner where you know sinners gather. Stay away from the
sarcastic and the mockers. Find God's footprints and take a
step in His direction. Spend time in His Word to learn the
things you need to know to continue in His tracks. Then
you'll begin to grow spiritually. Follow the Leader, because

He not only knows the way but supplies everything you need for the adventure of a lifetime.

You're surrounded by people who are all too willing to lead, so learning their character and where they are headed can be important information. You could be wasting time, walking away from God, or picking up habits that may take years to break.

Be intentional about finding the one Leader worth following. Choose to stop following anyone who wants your feet to walk in any direction that leads away from God. Learn to be a leader who is worth following because of who you follow. Be an example that helps others see God.

Anyone I meet is willing to let me follow them, God.
Not everyone is worth following, and only You walk a path
that's certain to lead me to the place where I was always meant
to be. If I follow You, then I can take what I learn and become
a leader for someone who needs to find Your footsteps.

DAY 61
Abandonment

Even if my father and mother abandon
me, the LORD will hold me close.
PSALM 27:10 NLT

The wound that holds your mouth in a painful smile doesn't tell the story that's in your heart. You might pretend that things are fine, but some can see through your grimace. You might entertain questions having to do with whether God will abandon you because you've been abandoned by others. Maybe one or both parents left you; perhaps your spouse divorced you; or maybe your grown children refuse to keep in contact with you.

Abandonment issues aren't just a family dynamic. You may have been abandoned by friends, dismissed by an employer, or rejected by neighbors. You may even feel abandoned by someone you loved who died unexpectedly. Lodge today's verse deep in your partially abandoned heart. Yes, these situations hurt, and God recognizes that people make choices to leave. He's very aware that not everyone who comes into your life will stay put.

God not only says that He won't leave, deny knowing you, or abandon you, but that He will hold you close. Let that sink in. When you're struggling to hold on after someone you love leaves, God pours on the compassion you need so you can catch your breath and discover that God's choice to love you has never depended on the choices others make. Can you imagine God saying that the only way He could stick with you is if everyone else did? When you've been abandoned, it's hard to trust the person who left. God will do for you what others haven't done. His Word gives proof that His love stands when you're listening to the footsteps of someone else walking away.

Do you want encouragement today? This is about as good as it gets. God knows you better than you know yourself, loves you enough to send His own Son to die in your place, and promises never to leave you or forsake you. Don't walk away from that.

When others give up and go, Father, help me remember You never have and You never will. Keep me close and keep me from being sarcastic. Help me to love others because You loved me first. Help me to show compassion because I see that in You. Let me not choose hate when I'm disappointed in others. Help me to remember that everyone needs You and that You don't abandon anyone even when they abandon others or have been abandoned themselves.

DAY 62
A Poorly Tuned Spiritual Engine

I want you to get out there and walk—better yet, run!—on the road God called you to travel. I don't want any of you sitting around on your hands. I don't want anyone strolling off, down some path that goes nowhere. And mark that you do this with humility and discipline—not in fits and starts, but steadily, pouring yourselves out for each other in acts of love, alert at noticing differences and quick at mending fences.
EPHESIANS 4:2–3 MSG

Older vehicles that didn't have fuel injection sometimes sputtered trying to get the right amount of fuel in the engine—failure was audible. If there was too much or too little fuel, the engine might make some racket and then begin to smooth out, backfire, or die. It was a frustration that often found the owner tinkering with the carburetor or fuel lines or putting an additive in the fuel tank. Most drivers would notice if their car was struggling just by listening to the engine.

Your walk with God can be a lot like a car with carburetor problems. If you follow too far behind or try to outpace God, it could be that your spiritual engine is out of sync. Your forward momentum is disrupted by a poorly tuned spiritual motor. Fits and starts can leave you exhausted. Your journey will be a struggle because you haven't paid as much attention to your engine as you should.

Of course you're not a car and you don't have an engine, but you are a human and you do have a heart. That is what we're really talking about. When you don't attend to the issues of the heart, your spiritual life will not run correctly. God is the mechanic that can set things right, but you might refuse His help or insist on trying to fix yourself. Both are bad decisions.

Make your heart available to God, make your hands and feet useful to others, and make up your mind to help in ways that demonstrate God's love for humanity. Don't let bitterness ruin your fuel mixture. God has given you a direction to go, so do what you can to be ready to go—and be ready to receive His help. Be ready to ask for help only He can offer.

Prepare that part of me that You made to go, God.
May my heart run well on the fuel of Your rescue, the help
of Your hand, and tune-up of Your Word. I don't want to
get comfortable walking alone. I don't want to get lost.

DAY 63
Desperately Seeking Clean Talk

Stop all your dirty talk. Say the right thing at the
right time and help others by what you say.
Ephesians 4:29 cev

Running on empty, running out of tune, and maybe running out of excuses. These things are all part of allowing your spiritual life to exist out of sync with God. God's principles as set forth in the Bible exist to help you diagnose when your life has degenerated into survival mode and away from the desire to thrive.

God's rules can become commonplace, and you may begin to think of them as suggestions. You come up with workarounds that further reduce their significance to you. You highlight the fact that God forgives, concluding that forgiveness is superior to obedience. From God's perspective, it's hard to transform a life when change isn't wanted.

Today's verse is one example of the way humans can reduce God's impact in their lives and conclude that it's okay. You might think that engaging in dirty talk is simply a way to remain relevant to people who don't know God. It's easy to think that people might accept your message of God's Good News if you sound more like them. You may even believe it's harmless fun.

But God is holy and calls for His people to be holy. His

Word says that what comes out of your mouth is a reflection of what is in your heart. The Bible tells you to "say the right thing at the right time and help others by what you say." God's man isn't supposed to tear down people with his words but build them up.

God not only doesn't mind if His family seems different from everyone else—it's what He wants. He doesn't say that you should blend in; He wants you to stand out. He doesn't say you should be cool; He cautions that others might ridicule you for things they don't understand about God. Nevertheless, there is something attractive about a person who makes it their highest priority to live a godly life.

I can't imagine You engaged in dirty talk, Father.
Your words show grace and compassion, not lies and rudeness.
Knowing that You are holy helps me get an idea of what
You do and don't want me to say. Help me to love and value
others enough to have the right words at the right time.

DAY 64
The Representative

You are a chosen group of people. You are the King's religious leaders. You are a holy nation. You belong to God. He has done this for you so you can tell others how God has called you out of darkness into His great light.

1 PETER 2:9 NLV

An ambassador is a representative of a country or an organization. What ambassadors say and do reflect on the country or company in either a good or not-so-great way. And you? Well, you represent God. You belong to His family because He rescued and adopted you. As an ambassador, you are to represent God well and to speak up and tell people how to be rescued.

Acting like just anyone in a society who doesn't follow God will leave you with no positive impact in the lives of others while making it seem like the best news you have ever heard has no value and isn't worth sharing.

If what you actually say is considered by others as speaking for God, does God sound very appealing, or are people confused as to whether you actually follow Him? Could they tell by your words and deeds that you have been rescued? Would they see or hear anything that would make them consider God?

Does bad behavior tarnish your position as an ambassador?

Do others see something in your life that makes God's claim of rescue seem less than life changing?

Being an ambassador would be very hard if you didn't have the full force and assistance of the God you serve. Get into His Word and get answers to the questions people ask. When you struggle, remember that God keeps the prayer line open. When you need help, He stands ready to assist. But when He asks you to do—or refrain from doing—something, the question He asks and the one you need to answer is "Will you do what I'm asking you to do?" The answer to that question might determine the ambassador you are, but it doesn't have to describe the ambassador you can become.

If I think You don't want my help, then I haven't been paying attention, God. People can first meet You by meeting me. Help me understand that what they see in me needs to look a lot like You. I represent You, and I want what I say and do to be useful in bringing people away from a life of darkness to the light of Your love.

DAY 65
The Light You Carry

"You are the light of the world. A town built on a hill cannot be hidden. Neither do people light a lamp and put it under a bowl. Instead they put it on its stand, and it gives light to everyone in the house. In the same way, let your light shine before others, that they may see your good deeds and glorify your Father in heaven."
MATTHEW 5:14–16 NIV

You have something other people need. They've been looking for it. They've seen the worst in people, the darkness that spreads throughout humanity and the selfishness that has roots deep in the human heart. They know these things exist because they witness them every single day. What they want to know is whether there's something better and more powerful available. They want to believe it's true.

They don't feel supported in their personal interest in changing the world. They've grown weary thinking things can never really change. They adopt a cause, stand in a protest line, or write a letter to someone they think has power over an issue they're concerned about; but at the end of the day, frustration descends like a blanket on them. Their efforts are at best reduced to a fifteen-second news clip or an "attaboy" from people who agree with them.

Christians are described as the light of the world. Therefore, people look to you for illumination on what's important and who you follow. Is your light hidden? Is it something you're embarrassed about? Have people stumbled because you've done your best to make sure people are distracted from its brilliance? What are you hiding?

This light that comes from a brilliant God is to be celebrated and shared. This news is exceptional, share-worthy, and the reason for your intended light show. Shine on.

Your light offers hope to those who think darkness is normal, Father. Help me shine like a lighthouse on the darkest night. May Your light bring understanding and compassion to those who have been confused and unloved. May it make me bold enough to make this my great ambition in life. May others notice You simply because I let them witness the light You've freely given to me.

DAY 66
Some People Don't Know

I am not ashamed of this Good News about Christ.
It is the power of God at work, saving everyone who believes.
Romans 1:16 nlt

If there's a better engine out there, you want to know. Then? You'll tell others about it. When you find a sports team worth following, you buy the merchandise and sing their fight song like a champ. If you have a favorite meal, you won't hesitate to describe its virtues and long for its appearance on your dinner plate. You get excited about the things that mean something to you.

What happens when it comes to your friendship with God? Do you get as excited? Do you share the news as much? Has your church attendance settled into a once-a-week habit or twice a year? Are you concerned that people will make fun of you if they discover you have made the choice to follow Christ? Do you feel that certain people would reject the Good News if you shared it with them, and if they did, would you feel rejected? That's a lot of questions, but maybe you could do the hard work of answering a few.

The apostle Paul boldly stated that the Good News brought to mankind through God's Son, Jesus, was not a message that should ever bring shame to the one who believes it's important enough to share. This message is more important than saying that the electric company will be supplying power to homes tomorrow. But that's how God's message is often treated. It seems like saying anything about it will be considered ho-hum. You might believe people will say, "Tell me something I don't already know." But some people don't know this message, and it's not old news to them. It's fresh, inviting, and extremely relevant.

When you start to think that people have already heard the Good News more than they want, just remember that for some the message is new, for others it's a refresher, and for some it will be just the right moment to make a choice that changes everything. Don't be ashamed. Don't stay silent.

Even if the news about You is something I've heard my entire life, God, there are some who have never heard, never believed, never considered You a choice. Give me the courage I need to open my mouth and speak of life change, new hope, and a great God. Let me express my respect for the greatest truth I can ever share, the greatest joy I have ever known, and the greatest love ever offered to me. Let me share with no shame. Let me experience no regret.

DAY 67
Be Taught, Then Teach

Jesus, undeterred, went right ahead and gave his charge:
"God authorized and commanded me to commission you:
Go out and train everyone you meet, far and near, in this
way of life, marking them by baptism in the threefold name:
Father, Son, and Holy Spirit. Then instruct them in the practice
of all I have commanded you. I'll be with you as you do this,
day after day after day, right up to the end of the age."
MATTHEW 28:18–20 MSG

Jesus gave the Great Commission because God told Him to. He assigned His followers something specific—to gather all the good things we know about God and take this information with us on life's journey to teach a class we were born again to teach.

What students will learn in your class won't be difficult, but it will require belief, and that's something you can't teach. Your students will either accept or reject class instruction. But just because this is true doesn't mean there's a loophole that gets you out of teaching.

Make this class mobile, knowing that everyone you meet is a potential student. And you aren't responsible for any student's reaction to what you share; you're only responsible to teach. As you teach, you should know that the God who taught you will be with you. He can help make the unclear things understandable. And while you may want to miss the teaching part, God will never miss any class that you teach, "day after day after day, right up to the end of the age."

Most people think that teaching is the job of a paid professional like a pastor or missionary. Some will even send in a check to help them do their important work, but today's passage doesn't make a distinction between a paid or unpaid teacher. This commission is for everyone—and that includes you. You have the opportunity to make God known to people who are lost without this Good News.

Be taught by God, and then be willing to teach what you know. You can learn something new every day so you can share—every day.

Because You made humans to be relational creatures, help me relate, Father. I know I need You. Help me tell others that You can be found, You offer help, and You will forgive. Some people won't hear if I refuse to speak the words that lead to life. Help me become the teacher You know I can be.

DAY 68
The Promise Delay

The Lord isn't slow about keeping his promises, as some
people think he is. In fact, God is patient, because he wants
everyone to turn from sin and no one to be lost.
2 PETER 3:9 CEV

Society is greatly focused on customer satisfaction. That's why there are free shipping and overnight delivery options. You expect promises from business owners that help you achieve your goals—on time. But sometimes they ship the wrong item or your order gets lost in the mail or an item falls out of the package somewhere along the way. That may not be the way the business owner wants things to go, but it happens. Their promises are made with great intentions, but they can't control everything that happens between their warehouse and your front door. Likewise, in life even the best person you know has never been able to meet every expectation and fulfill every promise, no matter how hard they try. No one can control everything.

Maybe you believe that God has fallen a bit behind when it comes to His promises. Many of the things He promised have come true, but not all of His promises have been fulfilled—yet. The word "yet" here is important to remember. Today's verse indicates that there is a reason some of God's promises haven't been fulfilled yet. For instance, He promised to return, but if He did, how many people would miss out on His great rescue?

If God waits to fulfill a promise, the worst-case scenario is that the promise has been delayed—never broken. And if His delay is intended to rescue more people, how patient are you willing to be? Do you have the same compassion for people who aren't even aware they need rescue? Are you sharing God's Good News?

Maybe God is waiting for His family to share the news so many need to hear. God's delay is not an admission of failure, but a gift of incredible compassion. His delay is an opportunity for you to share and for those who need to be rescued to hear.

While God's promise never depends on humans, He can use someone like you, who is willing to share the Good News to reach those He's waiting to rescue.

Your promises are true, God. If a promise hasn't come true, then You've made the choice to wait so that Your best plan can be experienced by as many people as possible. Help me learn that kind of patience. Help me appreciate Your compassion that delivers promises only when it's the perfect time.

Faith at Home First

Jesus. . .said to [the man delivered from demons], "Go home to your own people. Tell them what great things the Lord has done for you. Tell them how He had pity on you."
MARK 5:19 NLV

Your life story reads differently than anyone else's in history. Sure there are similarities, but there's a unique voice within your story that can reach someone else with God's exceptional news.

Before those who followed Jesus were commissioned to go and tell others all about Jesus, there was another instance where one man had his life story completely transformed by the Lord. After Jesus delivered him of demons, the man had no real idea what to do next. He asked if he could go where Jesus went, but Jesus gave him different instructions. This new directive sent the man home, not in defeat but as a key witness in a powerful new courtroom drama.

This man was given the task of telling his own family and others he knew what Jesus had done. He wasn't asked to grow the incident into a fish story—making it bigger with each retelling. He just had to share what happened to him with the people in his neighborhood. Among people who knew him, the story he told would have an impact because it was remarkable, unexpected, and transforming.

Jesus did for this man what the man could not do on his own—what no one who had ever met the man could do. Jesus quite literally rescued the man physically, spiritually, emotionally, and every other way imaginable. The rescue was immediate and complete.

Maybe this man needed time among people who knew him best to grow in his new faith in the Rescuer. The growth would be essential if the story he had to share would be something that reflected God and not something to make himself famous.

Before God sends you anywhere, He may want you to faithfully share His love with people you already know. Some people find it much easier to talk about faith with people they don't know. It may be among the bravest things you can ever do to tell your family about God. It may not be what they expect, they may be skeptical, and they may even ridicule you. Yet, as with the man Jesus delivered from demons, it may be where God wants you to begin telling the new plot twist in your personal story.

Make me brave enough to refuse to keep You a secret from those who know me best, Father. Before I go anywhere or do anything new, help me tell the people who love me that You love me too. Then let me tell them why.

Infants No More

*We will no longer be infants, tossed back and forth by
the waves, and blown here and there by every wind
of teaching and by the cunning and craftiness of people
in their deceitful scheming. Instead, speaking the truth
in love, we will grow to become in every respect the
mature body of him who is the head, that is, Christ.*

Ephesians 4:14–15 niv

Toddlers get into trouble. They don't have the experience
to understand certain dangers, and they're often in need of
intervention through the persistent care of an adult. If something looks fun or interesting, they toddle in that direction
and often get into more trouble. If an older sibling tells them
to do something, they will do it even if it means getting into
trouble. It seems toddlers and trouble go hand in hand.

Childlike faith has a benefit. Children find believing easier
than adults do. The downside of childlike faith is finding it
easy to believe anything. Some of the information you hear
and then trust could be incredibly wrong. As you grow spiritually, you learn to discern what to believe and what to reject.

Some people will work overtime to try to make you believe
something God says isn't true. It's possible that you've already
accepted some of their lies, but if you're growing spiritually,
you should learn God's truth and allow what you believe to

be transformed by the truth. Don't attempt to change what God says so you can continue believing something that's simply not true.

God wants all people who have accepted Christ's rescue to mature in their faith. You'll find it easier to grow when you spend time with others who also want to follow God. They can encourage you, and God can use their growth to help you grow.

Going where God is leading will be hard if you won't grow in the place where you are right now. Seek truth, speak the truth, and be willing to admit when you're wrong.

I'm grateful that I've learned to trust You, God. Help me to be willing to grow in this trust. Help me learn the truth and then believe what You say is the truth. I want to grow up in You. I want to find others who will help me in this adventure. I want to remember always that You have much more to teach me.

He Calls Your Heart Home

*Don't you realize that your body is the temple of the Holy
Spirit, who lives in you and was given to you by God?
You do not belong to yourself, for God bought you with a
high price. So you must honor God with your body.*

1 CORINTHIANS 6:19–20 NLT

You're familiar with the story of the three pigs and their
misadventures with home construction, right? One didn't
seem to know much about the enemy wolf and thought he
could live safely in a home built of straw, but it proved less
than reliable in the face of the wolf known far and wide as
Windbag. The second pig, instead of building a log cabin,
found sticks broken from sturdier limbs and made a home
that wouldn't pass any building codes. Windbag the wolf took
advantage of the second pig's miscalculation. A few huffs and
puffs later, that house was left to the kindling needs of the
community. The two newly homeless pigs made a beeline
for their third brother's house. By all appearances, he hired
an architect and spent the resources needed to build a solid
brick home, and let's just say that the end result meant safety
for the less prepared pig brothers.

Why was it important to retell a story you're familiar with?
As you spend time with today's passage, you'll understand that
you get to create the place where God lives. Your life is tied

to Him, and your body becomes the place where you connect with Him. You can make choices that diminish the quality of your life construction or choices that improve its quality.

God gave you life, and He paid the price to buy you back when you chose to sin. Your body will not last forever, but by taking care of it, you have more opportunity to use your hands, feet, and mouth to let others know about this quality life construction opportunity.

Your spiritual life is very important to God, and your physical life is also important because the decisions you make using the body you have can mean others get to know the God who calls your heart home.

I don't want to treat my life like it's an inferior piece of construction, Father. With whatever health I have, let me use what You've given me to share You with others. Let my life represent You to those I encounter. May I do nothing to bring shame to You and nothing that makes my life less able to follow Your adventure for me.

An Accurate Life Description

*It is obvious what kind of life develops out of trying to get your
own way all the time: repetitive, loveless, cheap sex; a stinking
accumulation of mental and emotional garbage; frenzied and joyless
grabs for happiness; trinket gods; magic-show religion; paranoid
loneliness; cutthroat competition; all-consuming-yet-never-satisfied
wants; a brutal temper; an impotence to love or be loved; divided
homes and divided lives; small-minded and lopsided pursuits; the
vicious habit of depersonalizing everyone into a rival; uncontrolled
and uncontrollable addictions; ugly parodies of community. I could
go on. This isn't the first time I have warned you, you know. If you
use your freedom this way, you will not inherit God's kingdom.*

GALATIANS 5:19–21 MSG

When you read through the list above, did you notice yourself? Did you remember how things once were for you? Did it bring a lump to your throat because you're struggling to find a different path that doesn't double back and leave you at the doorstep of painful choice?

This list puts a laser-sharp focus on the mess life can become. It demonstrates the contrast between the God life you have been reading about and the life you were meant to leave behind. Let's pull a list of words from these verses that are accurate descriptions of what you don't want to be: "loveless," "frenzied," "joyless," "paranoid," "cutthroat," "brutal," "vicious," and "uncontrolled." These things don't sound like anything you'd look for in someone you'd want as a friend. No one wants to see those things in you, but it's possible they have, they do, or they will.

You might believe that since Jesus came to make men free, this means you're able to do whatever you want. God forgives wrong choices, but He also wants you to recognize wrong choices before you make them. He wants His family described by terms that don't start with *loveless* and end with *uncontrolled.* The freedom God offers is freedom to make the choices that don't break His rules. Just because this is what people do on a daily basis doesn't mean that you're ever forced to do the same. He doesn't want you to. He's always had a better life description for you.

Doing the wrong thing is something I'm familiar with, God. I've made wrong choices, and I've seen them being made by others. Humans can easily connect to a list of painful choices. We like being selfish. You give me new opportunities to do things Your way. Help me accept Your opportunities.

DAY 73
The Better Description

God's Spirit makes us loving, happy, peaceful, patient,
kind, good, faithful, gentle, and self-controlled.
There is no law against behaving in any of these ways.
GALATIANS 5:22–23 CEV

Should Christians be recognized for their bad behavior? God never thought so. He knows that He's strong enough to bring new life to aging sinners. He knows that behavior modification will never be enough. If your heart isn't changed by His love, then you might be willing to do the right thing only until it's no longer convenient.

The best change God can bring is an inward change that affects all that you do on the outside. You'll always settle for too little if you just try to clean up what people see and leave the real you looking like an internal landfill.

You read the "bad choice" list yesterday and may be familiar with some of the items on that list. Here's a refresher of the low points: loveless, frenzied, joyless, paranoid, cutthroat, brutal, vicious, and uncontrolled. Compare that with today's list—the one where God is involved: loving, happy, peaceful, patient, kind, good, faithful, gentle, and self-controlled.

That's the stuff of best friends and ideal companions and the calling card of the trusted. With God, your choices can do more to leave you satisfied than making the choice to do your own thing. The things you do have been tried and declared a failure. God's list is complete with things that have always proven to highlight satisfaction and contentment.

The reason you let God have access to every part of you without doing your best to hide things you don't want to give up is because unless God has full access, you'll find a time and place to entertain things you were always supposed to leave behind. You might nurture a root of bitterness or a branch of division. You hold tight to a treasure trove of the seeds of discontent. You might call precious those things that can destroy you. But there's this better list described in today's passage. It's the promise of what's possible when you allow God's Spirit to do something in you that you can't do without Him.

I agree that Your list is good, Father. Help me long for this list to describe my heart. I'm not where I want to be and not where You want me to be, yet I can learn—and I am learning. Teach me to listen. I want to trust that Your better list is a perfect way to prove that You've been working on me. Please, don't ever stop.

DAY 74
Blending of Incompatible Things

Do not be joined together with those who do not belong
to Christ. How can that which is good get along with
that which is bad? How can light be in the same place
with darkness? How can Christ get along with the
devil? How can one who has put his trust in Christ get
along with one who has not put his trust in Christ?
2 CORINTHIANS 6:14–15 NLV

You exist in a world where you encounter people who don't include God in their thinking or take His rules under advisement. They make choices that they feel are to their advantage but may never consider how that decision might affect anyone else.

There's a disconnect between their thinking and yours. They may even be nice people who generally do good things, but their reasoning is different than yours. It can leave you confused.

If your beliefs about Jesus differ from those of another person, then it may not matter how likable they are. There will be times when you can't agree on certain things because they want to do something that goes against God's principles and you struggle with knowingly turning your back on God.

Scripture says not to make ties with people who don't belong to Christ. Like oil and water, believers and unbelievers don't mix. Good can't blend with bad. Light and darkness are opposites. Jesus doesn't have get-togethers with the devil. Trusting God will always have greater value and consequence than trusting someone who does not believe in God.

Paul wrote this passage for your benefit, and the reason may simply be that if you try to blend incompatible things, you will find yourself living a life of compromise. Living with guilt might become your new normal. When you feel separated from God by your sin, you'll likely leave God out of decisions that affect your future. But every decision you make can and should have God's fingerprints all over it.

The contrasts are everywhere—strong/weak, big/small, happy/sad. Living somewhere in between any of these makes you weaker, smaller, and sadder than God wants you to be.

You know the influence that people can have on each other, God. You ask me to keep a separation between who I am in You and who I let influence my decisions. Help me choose these close companions wisely. Help me choose You first.

DAY 75
The Temporary Housing Plan

[Jesus prayed], "I have given them your word and the world
has hated them, for they are not of the world any more than
I am of the world. My prayer is not that you take them out
of the world but that you protect them from the evil one.
They are not of the world, even as I am not of it."
JOHN 17:14–16 NIV

God's Word places a dividing wall between the things that would positively and negatively influence your decisions. Jesus prayed to the Father, saying that He'd given mankind His words, and the Good News He brought was not only rejected but responded to with unbridled hatred.

The disciples who believed Jesus' words became a target of hatred. If the disciples followed Jesus, and the world hated Jesus, they would be hated as well. The same goes for those who follow Jesus today. Jesus acknowledged that He was not a part of (nor was He interested in) adopting societal norms and standards. He also said that anyone who followed Him should not be linked to societal standards.

This is one of the passages used to declare that a Christian can be in the world but not of the world. You exist on the earth with people who have no use for what you believe in. Don't become like them, and don't do what they do.

You may not be able to buy every good and service from

a Christian, but you don't leave Jesus behind when you shop. You also don't condemn shopkeepers who don't follow Jesus for having a set of beliefs that differ from yours. Why? You can't expect them to live by God's principles when they have no idea what they are and have no conviction that they should be followed. To do so would be like being offended by someone who had no idea they were offending you and then you responding, "I'm upset. You know what you did!"

Because God's forever home for you isn't on earth, this world is essentially temporary housing while forever is being made ready. And because this isn't your home, you can expect people to be confused by your long-range outlook.

I need to be patient and share the news Jesus shared,
Father. It's news I know to be true, but I can't share
it if I trade hatred for hatred. You've given love when
I didn't deserve it. Help me give the same gift.

DAY 76
Experienced Sinners

We have stopped evaluating others from a human point of view. At one time we thought of Christ merely from a human point of view. How differently we know him now! This means that anyone who belongs to Christ has become a new person. The old life is gone; a new life has begun!

2 CORINTHIANS 5:16–17 NLT

You run a race, and in the end, there's a first-, second-, and third-place finisher. You play football, and there's a score that represents the final judgment on winners and losers. When a promotion is handed out, it is given to one person. This seems fair. It's expected. It provides a boundary for acceptability.

In life you look at any person and make similar judgments. They're either considered worthy or unworthy, winner or loser, and their past choices are the final judgment on their present acceptability. That's the human view, and very few people would argue with you, but then God enters the picture. When any person accepts rescue, their past performance is off-limits. If they're a new person (creation), then old judgment calls no longer apply. What was unacceptable when you resisted rescue becomes forgiven once you are rescued. Old evaluation forms can no longer be consulted to ensure you're not engaging with someone with a horrible past.

This is the way many Christians saw the apostle Paul.

He'd not been kind to Christians. In fact, he hunted them down and helped those who hurt Christians. But when Jesus rescued Paul, God didn't judge Paul as a criminal. God saw him as forgiven and treated Him as someone who could share His message. Paul did exactly that. His old life? History. His new life? Radically changed. You might find it ironic that this apostle would be the one to share God's message that proclaimed people should not judge new Christians by a past they left behind.

You're in the world. Make sure the world knows that condemnation doesn't define the life of a former sinner who has been forgiven because of Jesus' blood sacrifice on the cross for their sins.

I exist because people need to know You, God. They need to know that Your future for them isn't held hostage by their past. Sin always has consequences, but You've never met sin that You can't forgive. Thanks for removing the guilt of sin, the pain of separation, and the anxiety of being alone.

DAY 77
Time to Go Cold Turkey

Make a clean break with all cutting, backbiting, profane talk.
Be gentle with one another, sensitive. Forgive one another
as quickly and thoroughly as God in Christ forgave you.
EPHESIANS 4:31–32 MSG

Let's add one more layer to the unusual way the Christian life progresses. You don't judge those who don't follow God by the same rules that apply to those who do follow God. You don't respond to others based on their life before Christ. You don't scrutinize a person's past to decide what kind of Christian they'll be. Now let's talk about something you can do that will help you and the Christians you surround yourself with.

Christians are to be known for their love for other people—especially other born-again members of God's family. The apostle Paul taught that if you were used to making cutting remarks, if backbiting was standard operating procedure, and if you could list profane talk as a personal skill, then it's time to go cold turkey. Stop and don't go back. Let God replace all this rough stuff with kindness and care. Let go of the grudges that separate you from other people. Jesus forgave you, so you have no legitimate reason not to forgive others.

For Christians, the expectations change. What you did before you were a Christian was most often due to a lack of knowledge and also a lack of belief. If you didn't believe in

God, you had no reason to feel as if it made sense to obey Him. This condition didn't mean you were less guilty, just that you were less aware of your guilt. Growing Christians learn what God wants and then do what He asks.

The transition isn't just a try-to-do-better approach; it seeks to enhance God's instructions, improve willingness to obey, and steadfastly resist walking back to the man you once were. God never says you have to do all this alone. You do it by the power of the Holy Spirit, who comes to live within you when you commit your life to Christ. The same Holy Spirit who raised Jesus from the dead is now living inside you if you have surrendered your life to Christ. With that kind of power, the impossible becomes possible.

I've been rescued, redeemed, and reminded that You're my Father. You want to teach me, but it will be harder if I keep holding on to things You want me to release. Help me abandon my life mess in favor of Your cleansing. Set me apart to do what You've always known I could do in Your power.

DAY 78
Work Done Together

All of you are part of the same body. There is only one Spirit of God, just as you were given one hope when you were chosen to be God's people. We have only one Lord, one faith, and one baptism. There is one God who is the Father of all people. Not only is God above all others, but he works by using all of us, and he lives in all of us.
Ephesians 4:4–6 cev

Most people don't beat themselves up just because they can't physically do something that seems easier for others. The ones with the most courage will work on any physical challenge, either to learn a new skill or to do something in a new way. If you don't hear well, you might use your eyes more often. If you can't see well, you listen more. If your legs don't work well, you learn to use crutches, a wheelchair, or prosthetics. It doesn't help you to point to your own limitations and decide nothing can be done.

It's the same with the body of Christ. Each individual does something to help this body do something special for God. If someone is struggling, you don't just reject that person; you work with them to do what they need to do in a different way. Maybe you step up to help if you can, or perhaps you encourage other people to help get things done. Why? Every part of the body of Christ is needed.

In this body, the mind of Christ is the place where all members get their instructions, and there's absolutely no part of this body that He refuses to use. He's compassionate with the weak and lonely. He wants *you* to be compassionate too. Getting His work done together demonstrates how a well-functioning body of believers can champion unity, celebrate differences, and develop God's love among family members.

Abusing the body of Christ just because you don't like the way some members perform is less a form of correction and more a role of self-harm within the body. Discover compassion, kindness, and care. Then? Take them with you when you step in to help in the body of Christ.

No matter where I am on this adventure, I have let You down, God. I'm sorry. Thank You for not throwing me out when I failed. Thank You for sending others to help me. Thanks for Your forgiveness. Thank You for Your patience. Help me do for others these things that You do for me.

The Understanding Analyst

Try to understand other people. Forgive each other.
If you have something against someone, forgive
him. That is the way the Lord forgave you.
COLOSSIANS 3:13 NLV

God is looking for a few good analysts. Is that you? Pay attention to the messages you hear. See how they stack up with His truth. There's also another type of analysis you can do. God wants you to look at other people and see life through their eyes. Use their perspective. Then use God's perspective. Everyone has a backstory, and it often includes pain they're hesitant to reveal and reluctant to talk about. Be the analyst that kindly assesses their hurt and chooses soft answers. This ability to analyze isn't something you're born with. It's something God can nurture within your life. He can help you become trustworthy in the way you respond to the pain you encounter in others.

The snippy answer you receive from someone when you feel it's uncalled for may require you to understand them better and forgive them quickly.

Anytime you spend working to decode the responses of others can actually work to bring them closer to you. They may not think they need or even want a friend. Their actions and reactions may not seem inviting. You may want to believe them when they tell you to go away. But what they aren't saying may be the message you need to hear. They may want someone to see the value in their life, listen to them when they're overwhelmed, or just agree with them that life is hard. They just don't know how to ask for that.

You may be left to wonder why this is something you need to do. Can't people figure life out on their own? No. They can't. Life has a funny way of leading us to false conclusions. You can think you're owed everything or think you're entitled to nothing. You can have friends and learn that betrayal is to be expected. Life rarely turns out the way you want it to. It could be you didn't follow God's lead or that someone misdirected your internal map. The things you plan can change quickly. The problem is you might not be able to adapt as quickly as the change. If it's true for you, it's true for anyone you encounter.

You ask me to walk with others long enough to understand them, Father. Help me understand the struggle they live through so I know how to encourage and pray for them. Lead me to a place of kindness, and allow me to offer encouragement at just the right time.

A Tale of Reconcile

All this is from God, who reconciled us to himself through
Christ and gave us the ministry of reconciliation: that
God was reconciling the world to himself in Christ,
not counting people's sins against them. And he has
committed to us the message of reconciliation.

2 CORINTHIANS 5:18–19 NIV

Reconciliation is the restoring of relationship. The Bible tells the story of a father and son whose relationship went south. The boy left home and took his inheritance money with him. He blew it. Every last penny. People he met no longer wanted much to do with him. He was too proud to go home right away. He took a job, but the only job he was qualified for was feeding livestock. When he began to think the livestock feed was gourmet chow, that's when his pride released like an untied balloon. His new ambition in life was simply to get hired to work for his dad, because he knew that the people who worked for him were taken care of. But that's not what happened. As the young man walked home, practicing his groveling speech—willing to be called a servant and not a son—Dad spotted the wanderer and literally ran to meet him. The young man was accepted as a son without hesitation. That is a biblical picture of restoration.

Now think of yourself as the young man who wanted

what God could give but wanted your own freedom too. You ran from God, taking what you could. But misery gave birth to trouble, and struggle kept company with pain, and you suddenly realized you'd lost too much. You willingly admitted that even scraps from God would be better than living without Him, but then God called you His child and welcomed you back without a probationary period and without restriction.

Because this is what God does for you, He wants you to do the same for others. One of His great desires for you is to discover ways to help reconcile people to God, to help them establish or regain this kind of relationship.

God didn't just give the message of reconciliation so that you would be grateful, but so that this message would have such profound meaning that you would join Him in opening lines of communication so the lost might come home and be forgiven.

I find it hard to think of not knowing You, God. You've given me everything to live for, and You did nothing to keep me away from Your love. Help me to be reconciled to others and help them to be reconciled to You. Give me the opportunity and willingness to do this very important assignment.

High Roadside Assistance

*Never pay back evil with more evil. Do things in such
a way that everyone can see you are honorable.
Do all that you can to live in peace with everyone.*
Romans 12:17–18 nlt

Someone once said that taking the high road is preferable
because there's always a lot less traffic. You probably understand that. Being the bigger man means making decisions
that seem harder to make. It can seem impossible to extend
mercy when a clear injustice has happened. When evil strikes,
it seems to demand swift and immediate retaliation. Someone
has suggested that the choice isn't whether to get even but
rather how much to get ahead. This kind of thinking devolves
into civil wars within families and among friends.

God, who sees the end from the beginning, knows that
the end result of such an evil back-and-forth never really
benefits anyone and always hurts more than it could ever help.

On a practical note, the way you treat others is observed
by your family. If there are young ones in your family, they
see what you do and believe that your response is normal
and acceptable. If they see you retaliating, they will think
nothing is wrong with that and follow where your actions
lead. These young ones are just some who would benefit from
an honorable high-road response.

God wants you to live at peace with others and to inspire others to live at peace. You don't have to stress when things get hard, and you don't have to make life stressful for other people. Accept God's peace in conflict, and reduce conflict for those around you.

You will need *high-road*side assistance because you're bound to stall out with an overheated engine and maybe even brake failure. God's available plan provides the help you need when facing the choice you're struggling to make.

I can't find it in myself to back away from evil, Father. When I'm treated with evil intent, I want to believe a similar response is what's called for, but You tell me a bad response is never a good response to a bad response. Help others to know that You helped me make the hard choice to forgive and respond to evil with kindness. Your enemy hates it when he can't throw me off Your instructions. So, today I want to obey You in the way I respond to others.

Love Can't Be Passive

[Jesus said,] "Let me give you a new command: Love one another. In the same way I loved you, you love one another. This is how everyone will recognize that you are my disciples—when they see the love you have for each other."
JOHN 13:34–35 MSG

Faith is a matter of trust that links to the action of belief. You do something when you have faith. You make choices to love or to withhold love. You make the choice to forgive or withhold forgiveness—to give or keep for yourself.

When God gives a rule (command), you are required to do something about the rule—obey or withhold obedience. This can't be passive. Waiting to see if someone else will love people first finds you denying your need to be involved. You expect God to love you, but loving others may not seem to fit what you think of as a Christian's job description. You might pray for others or give to a fund used to support people. Both are great things, but if you never get involved, then you have very little reason to be connected enough to actively love other people.

This kind of action is not bragging about how compassionate you are, but it's an agreement with God that His plan to reach people is, in fact, reaching people. Loving others can seem like overhead speakers at an airport telling everyone that love is arriving on time.

God wants you to declare that His love is the change agent that everyone in this world needs. Taking out an ad online or in a print publication is nice, but there's nothing more impacting than love manifested through the actions of one person to the needs of another.

You can't just say, "I love people. I just can't stand being around them." God loves you in a very personal way, and His daily actions prove that this love is not hidden. It shouldn't come as a surprise that God doesn't ask you to just say the words "I love you." He wants you to take all you're learning about His love and use it to reach people who have always longed for that kind of love. God has given you what you need to love better.

Let me take action and love others, God. I want to fulfill Your command to love one another with obedience and joy. Your love is my example, and Your command is my motivation. Let Your love connect me to people who need love. May I make Your choice to love my choice.

Team Hypocrite

His words were smoother than butter, and softer
than olive oil. But hatred filled his heart,
and he was ready to attack with a sword.

PSALM 55:21 CEV

No one likes someone who says one thing but means another. It's called hypocrisy, and every generation has representatives. On the other hand, if you say, "Sometimes you just gotta play the game," it almost sounds like being two-faced or double-tongued is an admirable way of controlling people and managing situations. This almost sounds as if being a hypocrite is the only way to really get anything done, but is it really?

It's possible that today's verse is one you haven't read before, but it's a pretty accurate look at a hypocrite. Everyone knows someone like the man described in this verse. They can be a smooth talker with war on their mind. Their disposition is softer than oil, but their hand is on a sword. Hearing them say one thing but seeing them take action that doesn't match their words can be confusing. The word *betrayal* comes to mind.

People on team hypocrite may not want to speak the truth, but they also don't want people to lie to them. Some people complain that the church is full of hypocrites. The truth is, some hypocrites do go to church. They always have.

But this is actually really good news. After all, where else can they be exposed to truth written by a God who hates hypocrisy but loves hypocrites? Hopefully, they exhibit less hypocrisy the longer they follow God. Hypocrites are as welcome to accept God's rescue as anyone who breaks any other God law. Hypocrites aren't worse than any other sinner, and they aren't better. They're just one of many kinds of sinners who need forgiveness. So yes, they do belong in church. Yes, they can be forgiven. Yes, there is such a thing as new life.

If you've joined team hypocrite, it's time for a trade. You no longer need to try to remember how to act depending on who you're around. Let God help you be the same person to everyone. It's what He wants, and deep down you know you want it too.

I want the words I say to sound like the new heart You've given me, Father, but that won't happen without Your help. I'm so glad You're no hypocrite. You said You love me, and that has to be true because You don't lie. Thanks for accepting me. Thanks for agreeing to help me change into a man who is so much better than I once was.

Words, Beautiful and Horrendous

Men can make all kinds of animals and birds and fish and snakes do what they want them to do. But no man can make his tongue say what he wants it to say. It is sinful and does not rest. It is full of poison that kills. With our tongue we give thanks to our Father in heaven. And with our tongue we speak bad words against men who are made like God. Giving thanks and speaking bad words come from the same mouth. My Christian brothers, this is not right!

James 3:7–10 nlv

Wow. The things that come out of people's mouths! You've heard them, you may have said them, and you always wish they were words you never encountered. They almost blister your ears. You can control the urge to hurt someone physically, but words? They keep coming like a well-sponsored parade. Nasty words are unattractive, unwholesome, and very unwelcome. But nearly everyone says them. Few will apologize.

An animal trainer might be skilled at taming animals. But who can tame the tongue? It suddenly blurts out things you didn't intend to say, but you did and you will. These kinds of words often hurt someplace deep inside that no physical violence can match. You have been hurt this way, and you've hurt others using the same tactics.

You can use your tongue to form words of praise when

you listen to the radio or attend a worship service; yet there will come a time, often on the same day, when that same tongue will cut like a precision laser. How is it even possible for two completely different sets of words to come from the same mouth?

God wants you to know that it's time to knock it off. Words can be a primary tool of hypocrites. They are used by people who lie, cheat, and steal too. The list could get pretty long, because hurtful words are said by nearly everyone. On your own, you can't control those moments when ugly words rip from your throat and reach ears that never should have heard them. God can give you the strength to hold your tongue, alter your thinking, and choose a better response. You know that's not the way most people do things. But it's what God can do for you.

Help me think before I speak, God. Teach me how to moderate my speech. And remind me of a better way to speak. Thank You.

DAY 85
Angry Insecurity

A gentle answer turns away wrath, but a harsh word stirs up anger. The tongue of the wise adorns knowledge, but the mouth of the fool gushes folly.
Proverbs 15:1–2 niv

Two men lived on the same street, one old and the other young, one gentle and the other rough, one wise and the other foolish. You might think it was the old man who was gentle and wise, but in this case it was the young man. The difference in the two was that one was willing to learn and the other chose anger as a long-term response. People don't always line up with stereotypes. Young people may not always be rude, and older people may not always be kind.

No matter how old you are, God is willing to teach you how to be gentle, how to gain wisdom, and then to remember who taught you these things.

It's possible to spend your entire life stirring up anger and gushing folly and never learning from your mistakes. Such actions keep people at a distance and keep you from friendships.

While hypocrisy leaves you guessing, sometimes anger and folly do the same thing. These two brutes make people think you really are angry and foolish when you might just be working overtime to keep people away. It's easier to scare them away than to admit you're struggling. In fact, anger and folly often act as enormous billboards that tell anyone willing to pay attention that you're insecure.

Then again, insecurity takes up residence in everyone, and the only real remedy is God. Because He's in control, you don't have to be worried about the outcome. That will help decrease anger and diminish folly. Aren't you tired of entertaining these two?

To admit you're insecure isn't really news, and it shouldn't take anyone by surprise. In the middle of the night and in moments of uncertainty, a voice deep inside is telling you that you're not worth much and you can't really do much. You believe it's true, but you can't risk anyone else knowing, so you mask what you feel with an angry face and a volley of folly leaving your lips and damaging the people you should care about.

You can make me secure when I'm uncertain, Father.
I want to live in a place where I know You accept me.
And I need to be reminded that if I let You lead,
You have a plan that places me in circumstances where
I know I can be of use because You put me there.

DAY 86
The Itsy–Bitsy Dilemma

Trust in the LORD with all your heart; do not depend on your own understanding. Seek his will in all you do, and he will show you which path to take.

PROVERBS 3:5–6 NLT

One small spider with one impossible destination. This spider was persistent, and one by one each of eight legs was used to get to his destination. But just like the last time, this spider failed. The tunnel he climbed filled with water, and he was forced back the way he came in frustration. By afternoon the sun had dried his path, and the friendly spider ventured to the downspout and attempted to reach the roof again. Maybe this time he'd make it. But halfway up, the spider heard the crack of thunder and the steady thump of rain on the roof. This was just a different attempt with the same result.

This retelling may not be as magical as the children's song about a very small spider and his issues with a flooded waterspout. But in some ways, you're that spider looking to make gains on a different path. And every time you seem to be getting close, something happens that sets you back a bit. This usually happens when the path you want to follow is not the path God wants you to take. You think you know where you're going and how to get there, but the lack of progress is a hint that persistence alone won't get you where you need to go.

Maybe the spider missed the signs that told him to wait or stop. If he had, he could have avoided an unwanted spider bath. The best way for you to avoid setbacks is to trust God to provide directions. What you think is less important than what God knows. God wants you to trust His thinking, follow His leading, and obey His directions.

This not so itsy-bitsy dilemma is not the beginning or end of your struggle. You might believe you have a good idea about what you need to do. But *trust God first*. You might find you had the same idea, but if not, you now have access to a much better one—the one that God knows will work.

You have answers to every twist and turn in life, God. I should trust You before I trust what I think. If I doubt, let me doubt my thinking before I ever doubt Your certainty. Give me the wisdom to seek You, find Your answers, and follow Your path.

DAY 87
Not Like You

*"I don't think the way you think. The way you work isn't
the way I work." GOD'S Decree. "For as the sky soars high
above earth, so the way I work surpasses the way you work,
and the way I think is beyond the way you think."*
ISAIAH 55:8–9 MSG

Is God like you? You read the verses, right? No, He's not like
you. Maybe it's time to stop treating Him like He is.

God has always existed, and you had a beginning. He has
all He needs, and you need all He has. He can be everywhere
at once, and the best you can do is daydream about places
you'd rather be. He never changes, but you rarely stay the same.

Your best answers aren't God's best answers because the
way God does things doesn't look like they should work, but
they always do.

God is faster, wiser, and more compassionate than you
are, but He is also more patient and more peaceful, and He's
an excellent teacher. Learning from God isn't a matter of
improving what you already know how to do; it's learning
something altogether new using different thinking and fresh
obedience.

It doesn't make sense to treat God like a buddy. Yes, He
wants to be a friend, but because He's nothing like you, treat
Him with respect. He doesn't treat you like your friends treat

you either. He knows you better than you know yourself, and this knowing means that He'll never do anything—even unintentionally—that will leave you in a place He never meant for you to visit. That's a choice you make, but it's no decision that He has any part in making for you. He may give opportunities, but the choice is yours to accept or reject them.

He's a friend who just happens to be the Creator of life itself. He listens to your prayers because He's the Savior you've always needed. He's perfect yet sees your imperfection as an opportunity to model compassion. No, God is not the same as you. He doesn't act the same, make the same choices, or have the same mind. Recognize that you'll never be the same as God, and then marvel that this incredible God has done everything ever required to be your friend.

I don't want to treat You like You're just one of many friends, Father. You show up every day and offer life and share hope. You don't talk about what book You're reading because You've already written the world's bestseller. You don't have to ask what's in the news because nothing comes as a surprise to You. May I respect the incredible gift of Your friendship.

DAY 88
Filth Clingers

Turn to the LORD! He can still be found. Call out to God! He is near. Give up your evil ways and your evil thoughts. Return to the LORD our God. He will be merciful and forgive your sins.
ISAIAH 55:6–7 CEV

This God who can be known can also be found. He's not hiding, because if He were, He would never be found. Turn and look at Him. Seek Him. He wants to be found. You get to choose whether you'll seek Him. You get to choose whether you will call out to Him. You get to choose whether you'll turn away from a broken past for a beautiful future.

Many won't seek this God who can be found. They cling to the filthy rags that cover their lives. They believe that the tatters, bits, patches, and string that hold this morbid collection loosely is worth protecting. God can take all these useless outer layers, get to the heart of what's real, and tell you to take His new clothing, accept new life, and follow a new example. Yet some will hesitate to give up the filth that defined their spiritual attire and discover cleansing and forgiveness. The clothing God gives is clean, refreshing, and protective. Some people will act as if God is asking them to give up a treasure and will cling to scraps that should make their way to the trash can of failed ideas. They cannot loosen their grip, learn to ask for His help, or accept His offer of forgiveness.

Turn to the Lord! He can still be found. It's not too late, is it? Wait, you might believe it is, but remember that God is patient and He wants His rescue plan to be considered by anyone who will listen. This devotional may not be specifically for you, but you know someone who needs to read it. Let them.

The hand of a good God has been reaching, waiting to be noticed, hoping you'll say, "Rescue me!" God can be found. He's waiting to be found. The action you can take in this moment is to seek. You'll find what you're looking for. Mercy. Forgiveness. Rescue. Love.

Seeking You means finding You, God. Help me give up every other pursuit until I do. Give me a heart that can't wait to know You better. Give me a mind that can't wait to learn more. Give me a spirit that will listen to You. Give me a soul redeemed by Your rescue. I want to turn my attention fully on You. And when I find You, teach me the meaning of belief.

Trouble to Gratitude

We are glad for our troubles also. We know that troubles help us learn not to give up. When we have learned not to give up, it shows we have stood the test. When we have stood the test, it gives us hope. Hope never makes us ashamed because the love of God has come into our hearts through the Holy Spirit Who was given to us.

ROMANS 5:3–5 NLV

Visit any long-term care facility and talk to the residents. Everyone has met struggle. Trouble is a recurring visitor. Life seems like it should be easier, but it's not. The conversation might sound like comparing battle scars, but it might be more of a community sharing a common experience. Listen long enough and you might catch some glimpses of good things that happened following bad times. Children may have been born, marriages were celebrated, new jobs replaced old ones, and hope arrived even before trouble left.

God said that you should be glad for trouble. If that sounds like an odd statement, just know that God isn't hoping the worst for you. He's saying that trouble does something in you and through you that there's no need for if you only live through good moments and never experience conflict. Giving up isn't a good option. If trouble is a test and you survived, then you passed the test.

When hope comes, you're reminded that it's God who helps you endure hard times. It's God to whom you turn on difficult days. It's God who can somehow make bad circumstances become a good story worth sharing to the end of your days.

God's the perfect teller of your story. He's the author, and He doesn't leave a story unfinished. The struggles you encounter aren't meant to annoy you as much as they are to magnify His faithfulness. If no one lived through struggle, what kind of good news could you share? You don't live in a perfect world, and bad things will happen to all people. God can create new outcomes, but some people will be so caught up in thinking they should be immune from trouble that they become brittle and bitter, and their story seems to leave an unpleasant aftertaste you can't fully describe.

Choose to see trouble as a part of a bigger and better story.

I can resist trouble, give up in trouble, or blame You for trouble, Father. You simply ask me to endure trouble. You say that when I look at eternity, any trouble I face is really for a short time. You're faithful and will take care of me. Let me wait to see the full story before I ever give bitterness a chance to grow.

DAY 90
In Whom You Trust

Whoever dwells in the shelter of the Most High will rest in the shadow of the Almighty. I will say of the LORD, "He is my refuge and my fortress, my God, in whom I trust.". . .He will cover you with his feathers, and under his wings you will find refuge; his faithfulness will be your shield and rampart.

PSALM 91:1–2, 4 NIV

Praise exists because life itself provides the contrast between the trouble you face and the God who rescues struggling people. If there's nothing for you to be rescued from, then there's no need for God to rescue. But You do, in fact, need rescue—everyone does. Everyone faces struggle in their life journey, but only the wisest include God as a companion through each circumstance.

The man who wrote this psalm may have been Moses or David—each lived through struggle, hardship, and pain. But this psalm could be repeated by anyone who has ever lived through similar trouble—and that's everyone. When you understand what got you through dark days, you can mirror these words that describe God: "He is my refuge and my fortress, my God, in whom I trust." Did you pay attention to the word "trust"? You can't trust someone you believe has intentionally harmed you. You don't trust someone who doesn't keep promises. You won't trust someone who makes a habit of letting you down. But God? He can be trusted. He doesn't harm you, break promises, or let you down. Even when you struggle, God protects you from the worst of it. His assistance may be physical, emotional, or spiritual—sometimes all three.

You follow a God who never breaks trust, cares for you more than anyone else ever has, and doesn't abandon you in times of trouble. And because this is true, you can praise Him with words that describe your gratitude. Your descriptions of His goodness may be poetic but can never really capture how awesome He is, and your heart will seem to grow in the presence of His gifts of hope, kindness, and protection.

I'm on a journey with You, God. You stay close to me and protect, provide, and restore. May I bring honor to You by the way I speak about You, and may my words about You come more frequently. Lead me through the struggles, protect me while I struggle, and at the end of the struggle, help me share how You helped me survive.

He Is for All

Pursue righteousness and a godly life, along with faith, love, perseverance, and gentleness. Fight the good fight for the true faith. Hold tightly to the eternal life to which God has called you, which you have declared so well before many witnesses.

1 TIMOTHY 6:11–12 NLT

It was a motivational speech for the ages. The apostle Paul had written a letter to a young mentee named Timothy. This young pastor was an important figure in the New Testament because he was brought into a leadership position within the church even though he was not a full-blooded Jew. Now, God had made it clear that He loved everyone in the world, but most people still thought of God as the "God of Israel," or the "God of Abraham, Isaac, and Jacob." Those who were not Hebrew believed God's love was not available to them.

It's true that in the Old Testament God had called the Jewish nation a chosen people, but the sacrifice of Jesus was a once-for-all sacrifice. No one was left out of His rescue plan except those who refused to accept rescue. Some people liked being known as one of God's "chosen people," while others struggled to believe that God had opened the doors of His world to all people. Imagine young Timothy reading some of these final words of Paul's letter. Paul spoke of passionately pursuing faith, persistently waging spiritual warfare, and holding tightly to God's calling to eternal life. All of these things and more applied to Timothy, the young man who would have been thought of as an outsider just a few years before this letter was written.

The door had been thrown wide open, and Timothy was a poster child for God's love and acceptance. You're in the same position today. Take on the pursuit of God—nothing is stopping you but your own choice. Chase God's right living—it's for you. Believe in God's promises that apply to you—they will be fulfilled.

Your faith is accepted by God because He refuses to leave you out of His plan, away from His love, and without His presence.

I see separation between people, Father. This is a separation You did not make when it came to Your love. If I follow You, then I have Your example that refuses to be separated from people who don't look like me, don't live where I live, and like different things than I do. Help me accept anyone in pursuit of You. How can I withhold love from people whom You accept—people whom You love?

DAY 92
Be a Braggart

"Don't let the wise brag of their wisdom. Don't let heroes brag of their exploits. Don't let the rich brag of their riches. If you brag, brag of this and this only: That you understand and know me. I'm GOD, and I act in loyal love. I do what's right and set things right and fair, and delight in those who do the same things. These are my trademarks." GOD's Decree.

JEREMIAH 9:23–24 MSG

There are men who have won military medals of honor, yet those medals have not seen the light of day in years. For many of these former soldiers, the medal meant the loss of human friendship in battle. That loss is greater than any reason they can find to boast about something they rightfully deserve but have never felt the urge to celebrate.

You might expect boasting on the playground where boys size each other up and explain why they're the best at anything—from basketball to running, singing to blowing up a balloon, or art to math. But if there are winners, then there are also those who lost, and bragging can sometimes feel like salt dashed into an open wound.

You may have times when someone remembers something you've done and makes a big deal about it. You can't control what other people say, but you don't need to be the one to say it.

Today's passage does provide one thing you can—and should—boast about. *God!* You know Him and He knows you. Go ahead and name-drop in this case. Your connection to God means He's doing something in your life. He has shown you how loyal His love can be. He does what's right. He restores things. He's more than fair. *And you know Him.* Brag about that. Why? It's nothing that you've done. You simply tell others what God has done in you, for you, and through you.

Be a braggart—in one thing only—the goodness of God. Let others praise you if they choose to do so, but make praising God your answer to bragging.

I can brag about You, God. Let me start here, and let me say it now. You didn't have to rescue me, but You chose to do so. All I did was accept that rescue. You love me, and I love You too. But You started first so I would know what love looks like. You prepare a future for me that I can only accept; I can't make it possible on my own. You have always done what I can't and then have helped me do more than I could ever do alone. That's You. You're amazing.

Share by Doing

When others are happy, be happy with them,
and when they are sad, be sad. Be friendly with
everyone. Don't be proud and feel that you know more
than others. Make friends with ordinary people.
ROMANS 12:15–16 CEV

Your relationships with others are important. You can boast
about God and express gratitude for the good things people
have done for you because of the links they have to relationships. Focusing only on yourself and the things you're most
interested in does nothing to enhance relationships.

When good news is shared, treat it as good news. When
people hurt, you should hurt with them. Don't be standoffish.
Don't give people a reason to believe that you're convinced
you're the smartest person in the room. People don't need a
résumé to be candidates for friendship. Pair the following
paraphrase of today's passage with the Contemporary English
Version translation of Romans 12:5–16 above.

When good news is shared, treat it as good news. Don't spend
your time waiting for space in a conversation to share only
those things that interest you.

When people hurt, you should hurt with them. Refuse to
brush off things. If the hurt they feel is real to them, they
will need your empathy and support.

Don't be standoffish. This can seem like a nonverbal sign of bragging or saying that the other person isn't worth getting to know or appreciate.

Don't give people a reason to believe that you're convinced you're the smartest person in the room. This type of conversation will leave you talking to yourself about yourself. The other person will be looking for an escape plan.

People don't need résumés to be candidates for friendship. There's no person you could ever meet who couldn't use a good friend.

Each sentence is a bite-size nugget of encouragement and motivation—something you can do to build relationships with others.

Your wisdom is uncommonly good, Father. There's real practicality to Your words. Sometimes the logic of what You say is a bit like faith. I need to believe it to see it. Your plan for me involves relationships You want me to nurture—first my relationship with You and then friendships with others You bring my way. Help me to treat others with the same loving-kindness I receive from You.

DAY 94
Broken Pieces

Are you strong because you belong to Christ? Does His love
comfort you? Do you have joy by being as one in sharing the
Holy Spirit? Do you have loving-kindness and pity for each
other? Then give me true joy by thinking the same thoughts.
Keep having the same love. Be as one in thoughts and actions.
PHILIPPIANS 2:1–2 NLV

One benefit to asking questions is that they cause you to think about what you believe to be true. Today's passage is phrased in questions. You have to wrestle with where you get your strength, how you're comforted, whether you're experiencing joy, and how you're doing at building relationships. The apostle Paul knew that what you concluded would not only make your relationships stronger but would also mean that you might just find the right motivation to work with others and share the same love and feel the same joy as them.

You might get lost in what you feel is the soap opera of a failed life. You see the chipped and broken bits of your life scattered with every step you take, and you wonder if it's worth it to keep moving forward. Will another poorly placed step mean that everything about you shatters and leaves others staring at the debris of what was once your life? You may be convinced that you'll never be what you once were and that certainly you can never be more.

But what if you stopped looking at your own broken pieces and paid attention to what's going on around you? What if you championed God's work in other broken lives? What if you provided support to people who feel completely alone? See, here are more questions only you can answer.

You are likely recalling those times and places where God has supported you, comforted you, and repaired your broken pieces. And it doesn't even matter if you were broken at the hands of someone else or your own choices caused the brokenness, because God can forgive and He can repair. This is a message everyone needs to know. It's a message that can form in your heart, move to your tongue, and then make its way to ears that need to hear that there's hope for broken people. And it's that hope that brings joy.

Help me share the news that You fix broken people, Father.
I see evidence in my life, and I've seen it in others. Help me keep
from being silent about news people need to hear. Help me spread
Your compassion as Your kindness continues to change my life.

How Well Do You Know Him?

*Whoever says, "I know him," but does not do what he
commands is a liar, and the truth is not in that person.
But if anyone obeys his word, love for God is truly made
complete in them. This is how we know we are in him:
Whoever claims to live in him must live as Jesus did.*

1 JOHN 2:4–6 NIV

The scripture passages at the beginning of each devotional
in this book provide instructions, encouragement, and a few
warnings of what to avoid.

The Christian life isn't just a weekend experience at the
church of your choice. It's not just posting Bible verses online.
And it isn't the subject of conversation with nothing being
done about it.

Jesus isn't someone to simply be grateful for. The songs
sung about Him aren't just to be sentimental favorites. The
Bible isn't just an emotional connection to religion. The words
of the Bible are instructions for the life Christians should
be experiencing.

As a man, you grew up looking for examples. You may
have found an example inside or outside your family. It even
may have been a good example. Looking up to others is
something you may be very familiar with. Even as a small boy,
you may have looked at an adult you admired and thought

that someday you would like to be just like that man. This is what the Christian life is like. You have the perfect example in Jesus. You have information on how He handled situations. You can read the rules He lived by. Then? You can follow His example.

Today's passage essentially says that if you say you know Jesus, then you should act like He acted, do what He did, and share what He shared. It also says that if you say you know Him and act nothing like Him, then maybe you don't know Him as well as you think you do. *But you can.*

Pay attention to the way Jesus lived and what was important to Him. Then do that.

Your Son is my best example, Father. I can walk in His footsteps when I pay attention to what He did. I can act more like Him when He really becomes my best friend. Let my faith be more than a connection to the faith of people I have known in the past. Make it a vibrant life-giving faith that is abundant and leaves me free to follow You.

Do This Not That

Throw off your old sinful nature and your former way of life, which is corrupted by lust and deception. Instead, let the Spirit renew your thoughts and attitudes. Put on your new nature, created to be like God—truly righteous and holy.
Ephesians 4:22–24 nlt

You can buy an easy-to-assemble bookcase, but when you don't follow the instructions, you end up with something that looks nothing like the picture. You might assemble a toy and end up with extra parts and with it malfunctioning. New wooden patio furnishings might end up as expensive kindling for your fireplace. You see, instructions are meant to be followed. Ignoring them means never really getting the intended use out of whatever you're assembling.

God gave you instructions for life, but maybe you've never read them or have assumed that you learned what you needed to know when you were a child.

The Creator of life knew His creation might conclude they could make up their own rules, and that's what they did. So placing today's passage in His words of instruction provided the cautionary tale of why you can't make things up. Your past ungodly choices are to be rejected because they're riddled with personal desire and a bent toward deceit. Your past can't be improved or revised. It has to be rejected for something altogether new.

Following these instructions should leave you knowing what you need to reject, but what can replace this failed system of life choice?

What's next on God's to-do list? Well, because God's Spirit has been commissioned to stay with you and instruct you—if you're a willing student—He will reorder your thoughts and attitudes. If you've put aside your old nature, then it's time for you to fully wear your new nature. God made it just for you because you were made to make choices God makes. Life change is essential to a Christian—not before you can become a Christian, but afterward. That's when He can help, and it's when His Spirit can teach.

Your instructions say there's a time to let go so I can access what's new, God. My past can hold on with something like a death grip. Give me eyes to see that holding on to the past is placing a valley between myself and the new life You have for me.

Adventure Ahead

He handed out gifts above and below, filled heaven with
his gifts, filled earth with his gifts. He handed out gifts
of apostle, prophet, evangelist, and pastor-teacher to
train Christ's followers in skilled servant work, working
within Christ's body, the church, until we're all moving
rhythmically and easily with each other, efficient and
graceful in response to God's Son, fully mature adults, fully
developed within and without, fully alive like Christ.
EPHESIANS 4:11–13 MSG

You may get confused about how God works in a man like
you. You may believe incorrectly that He can't and won't use
any person who does not have credentials. While God uses
people with degrees in things like theology, biblical studies,
and children's and youth ministry, the degree itself is second-
ary to personal willingness in God's eyes. Spiritual gifts are
things you easily become good at, and it's all because God
gives people gifts they can use to benefit other Christians
and bring the Good News to people waiting to hear.

Not everyone gets the same gift, but the gifts God gives
means that your pastor isn't the only person who has a ministry in your church. Why would God give you a gift if He
didn't want or expect you to use it? Why would He equip you
if He had no expectation that this gift would ever be used?

There's a place for you in God's work. No Christian is ever directed to the sidelines and told that their job is simply to sit and watch. They're called to do more than observe and report. The Holy Spirit was sent to teach you a skill that you can uniquely use in the body of Christ. Accept God's good gift for you, and then use what He gives as His Spirit trains you for the adventure ahead.

God created the gift, supplies the instruction for your benefit, and guides you by His Spirit, but then you get to choose if you'll cooperate in sharing His gift that can be powerful and effective. The result is good—not because you did something special but because your cooperation through obedience means that God can do something special with your willingness.

Benching myself is easy to do, Father. I may not feel qualified to do anything special, but that may be why You ask me to do something that only You can do. When You accomplish any task through me, I can praise You because I know I have no personal ability to do what You can do through me.

The Mark of a New Life

*You have been raised to life with Christ. Now set your
heart on what is in heaven, where Christ rules at God's
right side. Think about what is up there, not about
what is here on earth. You died, which means that your
life is hidden with Christ, who sits beside God.*

COLOSSIANS 3:1–3 CEV

One of the greatest pictures of new life for Christians is the
death of their old life. What was normal for you in the past
no longer has to be normal because it is something different
than what you are right now. Even if you think this picture
is symbolic, it remains an accurate description and a defining
rite of passage for the Christian.

You accept a lie when you think that it makes sense to
somehow mingle your old life with your new. They're incompatible, and to try to live somewhere between makes you
ineffective in both camps. Both Christians and old friends
will wonder where you stand.

When your old life dies, your new life can begin. This
isn't like a light switch that you can turn on and off. It's not
like a dimmer switch that you can use to make it harder for
people to notice your new life. It's not even like a computer
program you can enter and exit whenever you want.

You're called to be *all in*. You left a life defined by sin to accept a life defined by acceptance and compassion. How is it even possible to be the same? Why would you want to be?

New life involves a shift in thinking. Instead of thinking about what you want and when you want it, you'll begin thinking about what God wants and the future He has planned for you. New life might be marked by kindness, compassion, and being certain there's a better day coming.

Because your old life is gone, you can accept its demise and move on to something that's so much better. You've accepted a new family, and God has accepted you. This can and should make a difference for you. It has made a difference for millions of others, and it's still making a difference today.

I can't embrace this new life if I'm not willing to bury my old life, God. Help me realize that the trade I received in rescue is not the death of a life that was good for me. Maybe I struggle because the old life is familiar and Your new life means change. I want to be certain that the change is worth rejecting who I was for who I can be in You.

DAY 99
Spiritual Adulting

"Do not fear, for I am with you. Do not be afraid, for I am your God. I will give you strength, and for sure I will help you. Yes, I will hold you up with My right hand that is right and good."

ISAIAH 41:10 NLV

Adulting is a term that describes the transition from acting like a child to behaving like an adult and doing things a responsible adult would do. Some colleges and universities have classes dedicated to teaching young people how to navigate this change. This can be a frightening time, because young people may be accustomed to a parent taking care of details that suddenly they must face. Initially, these young people don't feel confident that they can.

You may be in the midst of this altered mindset, or maybe you moved past it years ago. Something that might be described as *spiritual adulting* happens too. As a child, you hear Bible stories and believe in a good God; but in the act of growing up in your faith, you discover that there is more than just stories, more than just songs to sing, and more than a few verses to think about. There's a Bible to read, prayers you haven't memorized, and trust that feels like walking a tightrope without a net to catch you.

In those moments when you're taking some of these very specific adulting steps, God has some encouragement that assures you that He will walk with you and will catch you if you fall. He'll help you every step in this brave new stage of your spiritual adventure.

God vanquishes fear from this adventure. You need not feel anxious, because every moment is taken care of by a God who isn't distracted by what you do or don't do. He is fully involved in the individual plan He created for you, and He will redirect your steps to move you to a place where what you're becoming looks a lot like what He knew you could become.

Growing up is the logical outcome of faith in You, Father. I can trust You today and feel more confident in trusting You with new things tomorrow. I don't have to be frightened of the unknown because You offer the courage I need for every new step forward.

DAY 100
Plans beyond the Mess

"For I know the plans I have for you," declares
the LORD, "plans to prosper you and not to harm
you, plans to give you hope and a future."
JEREMIAH 29:11 NIV

In this final devotional on a trip through God's Word, you're invited to the story that inspired today's verse.

The people of Israel were warned that following God was the expectation and that failure to follow would result in a seventy-year time-out in Babylon. The people walked away and then stayed away from God. They ignored His warning. They chose their own path. God's response? He kept His promise and gave the people an extended time-out. God didn't use this verse to say, "You people are just getting what you deserve!" No, this God of love and compassion looked to the future and pronounced *good* over a people who'd chosen a bad direction. Read the verse again through the eyes of someone who had been told they would be made to leave their country and other people would tell them what to do. The life they had always known was going to change, and it was the consequence of their great "walk away," but God said, "I know the plans I have for you, plans to prosper you and not to harm you, plans to give you hope and a future."

What? This time-out was not meant to harm the people but to bring new spiritual health to them.

Maybe you've lived through the consequences of breaking a God law. God, in His miraculous mercy, offers forgiveness, but the consequences of sin usually remain despite forgiveness. You may wonder if God can ever bring hope to a self-crushed heart. He already has, and this book is proof that the messy things of life are not outside God's power to transform into good things. You may be in a spiritual time-out, but God's plan is to help you reach the other end of the struggle and prove that your future doesn't need to be defined by your past. God wants you to know that, even in your time-out, He'll never leave you.

I need encouragement, God. You bring it to my life in unexpected ways, and I'm grateful. Help me seek the encouragement in Your words and among Your family. Help me walk with You and stay close enough to hear Your whispers. Let me accept my life mess while I accept Your life help. I really am grateful.

Scripture Index

OLD TESTAMENT

EXODUS

15:2...........................Day 32

DEUTERONOMY

7:9............................Day 30
31:8...........................Day 10

1 KINGS

19:12.........................Day 1

PSALMS

1:1–3........................Day 60
23:4..........................Day 35
27:10........................Day 61
34:18........................Day 6
37:3–5......................Day 50
55:21........................Day 83
91:1–2, 4 ....Day 90
103:1–5....................Day 59
118:22–24...............Day 55

PROVERBS

3:5–6........................Day 86
15:1–2......................Day 85
17:27–28.................Day 43

30:8–9.....................Day 52

ECCLESIASTES

12:13........................Day 23

ISAIAH

26:3..........................Day 51
40:28........................Day 36
40:30–31.................Day 31
41:10........................Day 99
55:6–7......................Day 88
55:8–9......................Day 87

JEREMIAH

9:23–24...................Day 92
29:11.......................Day 100
32:17.......................Day 39

HABAKKUK

3:17–18...................Day 56

ZEPHANIAH

3:17..........................Day 37

New Testament

Matthew

5:14–16	Day 65
6:19–21	Day 53
11:28–30	Day 7
22:37–38	Day 21
28:18–20	Day 67

Mark

5:19	Day 69

Luke

10:40–42	Day 20

John

13:34–35	Day 82
17:14–16	Day 75

Romans

1:16	Day 66
5:3–5	Day 89
7:24–25	Day 11
8:1–2	Day 12
8:26	Day 4
8:38–39	Day 9
12:2	Day 19
12:12	Day 28
12:15–16	Day 93
12:17–18	Day 81

15:4	Day 18

1 Corinthians

6:19–20	Day 71
9:19–23	Day 47
10:13	Day 33

2 Corinthians

4:16	Day 13
4:17–18	Day 8
5:16–17	Day 76
5:18–19	Day 80
6:14–15	Day 74
9:8	Day 58
12:9–10	Day 34

Galatians

2:21	Day 17
3:28	Day 46
5:19–21	Day 72
5:22–23	Day 73

Ephesians

2:8–9	Day 15
2:10	Day 14
4:2–3	Day 62
4:4–6	Day 78
4:11–13	Day 97

4:14–15....................Day 70
4:22–24....................Day 96
4:29...........................Day 63
4:31–32....................Day 77

PHILIPPIANS

1:6..............................Day 29
2:1–2........................Day 94
2:3–4........................Day 24
3:7–8........................Day 57
3:13–14....................Day 2
4:6–7........................Day 27
4:11–13....................Day 49

COLOSSIANS

1:9..............................Day 44
1:16–17....................Day 22
2:8..............................Day 3
3:1–3........................Day 98
3:13...........................Day 79
4:5–6........................Day 45

1 TIMOTHY

2:1–4........................Day 26
6:10–11....................Day 54
6:11–12....................Day 91

2 TIMOTHY

3:16–17....................Day 16

HEBREWS

4:12...........................Day 38

JAMES

1:5–8........................Day 42
3:7–10......................Day 84
3:14–16....................Day 40
3:17...........................Day 41
4:1–2........................Day 25

1 PETER

1:8..............................Day 5
2:9..............................Day 64

2 PETER

3:9..............................Day 68

1 JOHN

2:4–6........................Day 95
2:15–16....................Day 48